WE Summit Together

*A Collection of Empowering Stories
by Empowered women.*

First Published in 2019 by
Success in Doing Publications

Copyright © Donna Kennedy, 2019

The author asserts her moral rights.

This book is sold subject to the condition that it shall not, by way of trade or otherwise, be lent, resold, hired out or otherwise circulated, without the publisher's prior consent, in any form other than that in which it is published and without a similar condition including the condition being imposed on the subsequent publisher. No part of this publication may be reproduced or transmitted in any form or by any means, electronic or mechanical, including photocopying, recording or storage in any information or retrieval system without prior permission of the publisher in writing.

www.wesummit.ie

ISBN: 978-1-9160176-0-3

Contents

- Foreword 5
- Introduction 8
- You are Enough 28
- It's OK! 51
- Overcoming Obstacles, Despite Limitations 71
- Change and Letting Go 93
- Claiming back Your Power 115
- Respect and Self-Worth 140
- Loving yourself 163
- Unleashing the Silent Hero 180
- Purpose 197
- Living Life to Your Values 221
- Be a W.I.T.C.H 239
- Courage 269
- Happiness and Gratitude 281
- A Final Note 303
- Acknowledgements 306
  - About the Authors 307

Foreword
by
Christina Noble, OBE

I met Donna Kennedy when I was invited to speak at one of her seminars, the Women's Empowerment Summit. I found her to be a caring, sincere and professional woman, a woman with a wealth of experience who has helped others based on her own life experiences. This qualifies her to empower others to overcome all obstacles that stop them from reaching their own goals in life and above all to find real happiness and to love themselves. Love is the most powerful force we have. Sometimes we might have to search our souls to find it, but it is there, and when we connect with it, it can enrich our lives and make us whole again.

It's easy to feel alone in this world, but you are not alone. There are people here to support you, just be open to it. Of course, nobody is going to do it all for you as there are decisions and choices that you must make for yourself. There is no point in sitting around saying, "Poor me". Instead choose to get up and tell yourself "This is my life" and give it your all. You are here for a reason and you have a purpose. Choose to find your purpose and acknowledge it. When you do, you will have peace of mind, which is a magical feeling. Just believe in yourself.

When I was a child, I was surrounded by cruelty of the darkest kind, and at times I felt like giving up, but something stronger within me told me to never give up. The love I had for my brothers and sisters was greater than any negativity or obstacle. It kept me strong and made me determined. I did what I could to make sure we survived, and I told myself, "I can do it, I must do it, I *will* do it!" And we survived.

Later in life, I felt that same maternal love when I had my own children and I was determined to make sure they grew up to be healthy and happy people, against any odds. They are now all healthy, happy and well-educated, and they all have their own homes. When you have love and determination, anything is possible. Just don't give up.

Love has such power. It has led me to serve the needs of vulnerable children across the world. It has given me the determination to empower impoverished communities with sustainable futures. I have come up against obstacle after obstacle, but I always remind myself that love is stronger, and I find a way. In the last 28 years the foundation I established has implemented 164 projects that have helped over a million people lead more empowered lives.

You see, when you become determined and connect with the powerful love-force that is within you, you can do anything. If you have bad days, use them to clear your mind and carry on, but never give up. You are worth more.

Use the information in the book to find what it is you are truly passionate about and do what you love. The only way is up!

Introduction

by bestselling author, Donna Kennedy

Have you ever had that feeling where you know deep down that you have so much more potential, that you have so much more to give and be, yet for some reason you just don't seem to be able to make things happen the way you want? The doubts, the worries or the obstacles always seem to linger in the background and hijack your plans and efforts to create the life you truly desire and deserve. The truth is, we all have, even those "perfect" people who seem to have it all worked out. We've all danced with fear and doubt, and as a result it's easy to forget our own unique moves and abilities, our own innate sparkle and our ability to shine confidently in our own right. Let me tell you this now, you were not born to play small or recoil in the face of your brilliance. You were born to shine!

You were born to be the best version of yourself, not a limited version of yourself or a shadow of someone or something else. You were born to find and ignite the magic that is within you and utilize it, so that you can lead a fulfilled meaningful life and feel proud to share the joy that brings with those that matter most to you. In this book, my co-authors and I would like to empower you to do just that. Through our stories, experiences and life lessons we will show you that the life you want is possible. We have come into your life to support you and empower you to summit to new heights. From this point on, you are not alone. We are happy to support you here, and it is our belief that we achieve much more when *WE Summit Together!*

Just imagine for a moment, imagine being the best version of yourself. What would that look like? What would it feel like? No fearful hesitation, second guessing or self-criticism, just love and acceptance of yourself. What would a life like that sound like? Maybe you would speak nicely to yourself, instead of putting yourself down. How fabulous would it feel to believe in yourself and feel securely confident, knowing that you have real value? Wouldn't that just be amazing!

Now take it a step further and imagine what you would do differently, if you felt more empowered to be the best version of yourself. You know those things that you would just love to try but have been putting off because of discomfort or fear of what other people might think or say, for example. You know those things that you would love to try, if only that doubting monkey would get off your shoulder? Well, from reading this book you will realise that you can lead the life you want, no matter what your current circumstances or beliefs.

How do I know? I am living proof of it. And for the purposes of this book, I will share some of my story with you, so that you can be confident that the information in this book, when applied, has the potential to transform your life in the most wonderful way. It goes beyond theory. It's real.

Disempowerment to Empowerment

Today people see me as a confident successful leader. Indeed, I am leading the amazing ladies in this book. I speak on stage to thousands of people, empowering them to have the courage to be their best selves. I appear on TV and radio regularly without any fear. When I walk into a crowded room I do so with ease and joy. I do not compare myself to anyone. I feel secure and good enough just as I am, and I love nothing more than to see people succeed and be happy, including myself. That's great, right? Absolutely! However, it wasn't always so great.

At one point, my life was nothing more than a fearful existence. I feared everything and everyone; even talking to people I knew was difficult. My confidence was on the floor and I was utterly miserable. I know that may seem hard to believe, considering where I am today, but the woman I am today is very different to the woman I once was. I have no desire to impress you with that fact, I want to impress upon you that if I can create a life that allows me to feel empowered and amazing, you certainly can. Everything you want is totally possible!

I will share something personal with you, something I haven't shared in any of my previous books, but something I think will help you see just how possible it is to have the life you want, no matter how bad things are or how disempowered you feel.

A letter from my late mother

It was a mother's worst nightmare to watch her beautiful precious child suffering anorexia.

At first, I didn't know she had the illness. I did notice that she wasn't eating very much but I thought it was a teenage phase. Donna was the fifth of seven children and at that time the fashion was sloppy jumpers and jeans, which hid a lot.

The first time it dawned on me that something was wrong was on a shopping trip to buy clothes. One of her sisters noticed how thin Donna was when she tried on clothing and she told me. The warning lights went on and I was vigilant from then on. I noticed how secretive she was around food, sometimes only eating a couple of apples for the whole day.

I brought Donna into the G.P. for a check-up and the doctor explained anorexia to me and how Donna felt she had no control in her life and this was her way of exercising some sort of control.

I talked to Donna and we tried to work out some sort of diet that she was comfortable with. She agreed to take a bowl of porridge in the morning and have a yogurt with her apples. It was a start.

I tried to get her to eat but I had to watch very closely because if she got the chance she would go to the toilet and vomit. Her weight went down to 31kg (5 stone), which is famine weight for a girl of 1.7 metres (5'10") in height. Her pelvic bones stuck out and there was nothing but a layer of skin covering bone. She looked like a skeleton but all she could see when she looked in the mirror was fat.

I had some cameras that developed photos instantly and I took a photo of her pelvis and gave her the photo. I thought she might be able to see in the photo what she couldn't see in the mirror. When she saw the photo, she started to cry. She said she looked like a hippo.

It was so scary. Thinking about it now I can feel the sickening fear that was tearing my heart out of my chest. I felt so helpless and yet I could not give into that feeling. I prayed so hard every day for the strength to know what to do and for the patience and energy to keep going and to help my precious child to walk through the illness and gain her life.

I brought her into the G.P. again. Donna's blood pressure had gone dangerously low, her heart was failing, and she needed to go to hospital. After a week in hospital her weight had dropped by another 7 pounds, despite the best efforts of the hospital staff. My G.P. suggested that I stay with Donna during the days and try to get her to eat. She was almost dead. So, I got up every morning at 7am and made her a bowl of porridge and then her Dad drove me the twelve miles to the hospital. I stayed with her for the day until 8pm and I did this every day.

During the day I fed her and watched that she did not try to vomit under the sheets. I would read to her and a lot of the time she slept because she was so weak. She even went into two mini comas during that difficult time.

But gradually Donna got better, and we were able to bring her home. There was still a long way to go and I kept praying for strength, patience and understanding. One of the most difficult times was when she would literally want to disappear. Her bedroom at the time had a bed beside a wall and she would put her head and shoulders down between the bed and the wall and the most horrible moan would come out of her. My heart nearly broke hearing that sound. It illustrated exactly how she was feeling inside. For a mother to hear that sound from her precious child is not something that any human being should experience. I prayed for help and then I forcibly took her out of the "hole" that she had made between the wall and the bed. And I would lay her down to stop her trying to get back into the hole. Then I would just hold her. I loved her so much.

It took Donna a long time to get better. When one is an alcoholic one speaks of the demon drink. It is very apt because with any addiction there is a demon attached *to it. The demon anorexia lurks in the shadows waiting to gain control again. Doctors speak of anorexia as the way a person gets control in their life. But I know this to be flawed thinking. The person loses control to anorexia behaviour, which controls the person, almost to death in Donna's case. The only way a person can have any real control in life is to leave negative thoughts behind and never allow them into one's life again.*

I remember the day I came out of a coma. I was on death's door. I blubbered tears of desperation in my mother's arms. I was hopelessly miserable, I didn't want to be that way, but I couldn't see a way forward. It felt like I was being magnetised to stay where I was, in my box of misery, even though I hated it. Ironically, staying where I was made me feel safe. Controlling my body made me feel safe. I didn't like it, and I really wasn't in control, but it felt safe to think I was. To get better meant I had to give that up. That was a petrifying concept, yet to others it seemed so easy. "Just snap out of it, eat and live happily ever after. The end." If only it was that easy. In my case, logic didn't even come into the equation. It was like I was emotionally hijacked and unable to engage in logic. Nothing made sense, and nobody understood why I found it so hard. How could I expect them to? I refused to speak about it.

Living on a knife edge, in the space between life and death, I knew that it had reached a point where I had no choice but to speak about it. If I didn't, I would die as my body was failing. Crying and afraid, in my mother's arms, I took a deep breath. I can still remember how physically painful it was to take that breath in preparation for what I was going to say. I didn't want to say it, but I had to say it, if I was to get better. And at that I told my mother about what happened when I was seven years old and how it had been eating away at me – literally.

I had been sexually assaulted by a stranger who came to our home to visit. Nobody in my family knew. Nobody could have known as I hid it well, although they had noticed that I went from being a happy little girl who sang happily in the back garden to being distant and withdrawn and crying for no apparent reason. I couldn't cope or even process what had happened at that time. It was easier to lock it in my mind. I didn't want anyone to know about it as it made it too real. I figured that if I hid it, I wouldn't have to talk about it, and it would make it go away. I could just pretend it didn't happen, bury the feeling, and get on with my life somehow.

In hindsight I coped by controlling the numbers on the weighing scales, my desperate attempt to regain control of my body.

Seeing the numbers go down was a visual comfort for me. It told me that I was in control of my body again, that I had a defence around me that nobody could tear down or take away from me. It also meant that I was punishing my body, hurting it and destroying it, which I thought I deserved. I hated my body for what had happened, even though I wasn't responsible for it. I wanted it to disappear. How was I supposed to give that up?

With tears of pain in her eyes my mother hugged me that day and we cried together for a long time. She held my wet face and looked at me "Donna, I don't know what to do but I prayed about it. What can we be grateful for right now?" My mother always turned to prayer when it came to needing answers, but I thought her question was ridiculous, cruel even. Grateful? What did I have to be grateful for? She should have been consoling me, not telling me to be grateful! Was she out of her mind?! I felt patronized and angry at the deepest level.

However, she looked hopeless and it gave me a horrible pain in my heart to see her that way, so I took another deep breath and decided to listen. "Sweetie, please do what I ask. We are at a place of desperation, a place where we must do something good for you now, no matter how bad things have been up to now. I don't have the answers, but I have prayed. Right now, I want you to tell me ten things that you are grateful for. Let's write them down."

At that moment my mind felt like it had been thrown in a tumble drier at high speed. I felt so angry to hear her words of "wisdom". Attempting to compose myself, I held my breath and bottled how I was feeling. I couldn't *not* give her logic a chance. I loved her so much, so I trusted that there was a valid reason to why she was asking me to do this ridiculous exercise. Honestly, I couldn't think of one thing to be grateful for, never mind ten!

"I'll start you off. Look at your hands. Imagine life without your hands." Okay that was one thing I could be grateful for I suppose. I certainly wouldn't like to lose my hands, I thought.

"And what can you do with your hands. You're good at art, aren't you?"

We sat on my bed for some time discussing what I could be grateful for. I now understand that my mother was desperately searching for my strength, even a glimmer of hope that she could grab on to and pull me up. She hoped she might find it in gratitude. And she did. I had forgotten how precious my life was, how precious and strong I was. She was reminding me of the value of my life, to give me a foundation to build on and recover.

The Moment of Change

People often ask me was that day of gratitude the pivotal moment of my recovery, and until very recently, I always thought it was. Reading the above, it's easy to see why, because things did change on that day. However, recently I was asked to give a talk about the topic of Gratitude at a conference, so, as I do in preparation for any of my talks, I reflected on how best to get my message across to the audience.

On reflection, it dawned on me that although gratitude was a massive catalyst for my recovery, something tiny came before it that ignited the whole recovery process. In fact, it was so tiny that until my deliberate reflection, I had missed it. What I am about to tell you is, in my opinion, the catalyst for all life transformation.

It dawned on me the night before my talk, I was lying in bed and I couldn't sleep as my mind was busy thinking. I tossed and turned as I tried to get to sleep but it just wasn't happening. Then out of the blue, the word BELIEF flashed in my mind. 'Mm that's weird.' I thought to myself. Then it flashed in my mind again, and then again. It was like an internal movie-still that just lit up in my mind. Its persistent repetition became annoying so, in an effort to get it out of my mind, I picked up my phone, opened my Memo App and typed in the word BELIEF. Then, for whatever reason, I just wrote the word BREATH beside it. I have no idea why, other than I felt compelled to write it. Odd I know!

Putting the phone back on my bedside locker, my mind still felt too busy to sleep, so I decided to write whatever came to me until I felt sleepy enough to go to sleep. I looked at the words I had written, BELIEF and BREATH, and it suddenly hit me like a brick in the head; although gratitude was essential, my recovery was not just because of gratitude. It was because of a *belief in a breath*.

Looking back, it all happened in those two deep-breaths that I forced myself to take that day. The first deep-breath was taken to help me tell my mother about what had happened when I was seven. The second deep-breath was taken when I chose to contain an emotional outburst when she asked me to be grateful for my life. That breath, that tiny space in between "do or don't", "live or die" is where the real change happened. The gratitude followed my decision to be open to change within that space. That space holds *decision* and it is only in decision that we choose to make change, to take action or stay stagnant, to continue living or to stop breathing and die. In that breath I decided to listen and become open to something new, to create a new belief about myself and my life.

Think about it in general terms for a moment. When most people are in a situation where a big decision is necessary, it's not uncommon to take a deep breath, usually without realising we are doing it. We do a 1-2-3 countdown or something similar, in preparation for that decision. We *pause, decide and then take action*. Do it now. Take a deep-breath in, and before you breathe out hold the breath for a second. Become aware of the holding space between the inbreath and outbreath. *THAT* is where it all happens, that space allows for the decision to empower everything, even our survival.

No sooner had I realised this than the word BELIEF flashed in my mind again, but this time I bizarrely became aware of the centre of the word and I saw a box around it. Again, there was no reason why, it just popped up. Within the word belief is the word LIE!

The word lie was trapped within that box, like I used to feel trapped in my "comfort box" of misery. I thought back to before I made my decision to listen to my mother and get better. I had in fact been living a lie. I had told myself everything bad that ever happened to me was my fault. I had told myself that I was a horrible person and that nobody liked me, that I didn't deserve to be happy etc., all sorts of rubbish that kept me stuck. To get better I had to drop the defence and move out of that box of comfort (beliefs). I needed to create a new belief about myself and my life, even if it felt uncomfortable and not within controlled boundaries. The truth is, the only reason I was afraid and felt patronized and angry "because of" my mother, was because my comfort box was being rattled. I wasn't used to that and I didn't like it. When it was rattled, I had the option of reacting (positively or negatively) or staying where I was. But it was only by *deciding and moving out of* the comfort box that I could take positive new action.

Let's look at the word BELIEF a bit more now, and let's create some motion around the box to see what happens. We will rattle it simply by moving one letter, the letter E. Watch what happens to those lies and those beliefs when we rattle the lie and create a tiny bit of motion.

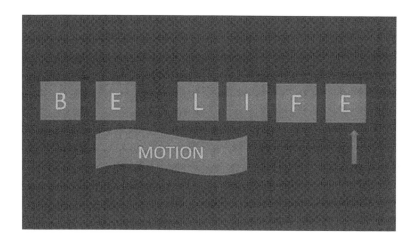

BE LIFE - We become life!

A simple shift in movement can be the catalyst for all sorts of wonderful change. In this case, it was just a matter of moving the letter E.

Interestingly, in Latin, the letter E denotes "out". Now let's see what happens when we create motion around that E (out).

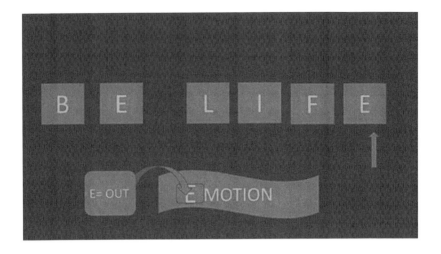

It becomes E-MOTION! And what is emotion only a charged-up feeling as a result of movement. This would explain why I became so angry when my mother tried to move me out of my comfort box and into a new belief!

Strangely enough, if we look at the kind of words that we associate with any change, especially positive ones, they have something in common. Think of a goal. Isn't it fair to say that the following words are words we might associate with goal achievement?

Motivation	Negotiation
Decision	Production
Collaboration	Assertion
Determination	Manifestation
Co-operation	Expression
Emotion	Passion
Organisation	Realisation
Magnification	Actualization

Now look closer. What do you notice about all these words?

They all contain the word ION, i.e. a charged particle of movement. Therefore, *movement* is essential for all change to occur. We must move out of our comfort boxes, our liwmiting lies and old stagnant beliefs, and into something new.

Play and Explore

When we come into this world, we are naturally excited to reach our potential. We play. We move. We are curious and excited about learning new things. We don't sit still, and we don't get stuck in limited thinking. We just explore and search, even in the simplest of situations. We ask questions. We try new things and we feel proud of ourselves when we achieve new milestones. In fact, when we do, we are praised and celebrated by the people around us.

However, as we get older the novelty wears off and the excitement dwindles. Instead of continuing our adventure of learning more about our potential, we stop playing, we recoil, slow down, and "fit into" the comfort boxes bestowed upon us by the people and things in our environment. We become *environmentally conditioned*. Our behaviours, our habits, our beliefs, even our accent, are like downloaded scripted programmes from our environment. "You should do this, and you shouldn't do that.", "Don't get too big for your boots", "Who do you think you are doing that?", "The person down the road did that and it didn't work out.", "Having the ideal partner only happens in fairy tales." etc. And so, we place ourselves on pause mode and decide (consciously or unconsciously) that it's "safer" to stop moving in the direction of what we can be and fit into the comfort boxes of what we should be.

Think of it like a scripted movie and you are the director. In front of you, you have a bunch of scenes acted out by "professional" actors. Obviously, in order to create a movie masterpiece, you must choose the scenes you want and dump the ones you don't want, and to see it unfold you must *play* the tape. Let's say you've selected your scenes and you play the tape. Everything looks great. You feel excited and proud, but then suddenly the images freeze on the screen. You try to fix it, but it remains a frozen movie-still, what's worse it's paused on a scary scene. You get frustrated because you can't see the movie, and you start shouting at the people around you.

Then I turn to you and whisper in your ear, "You have your finger on the pause button. If you want to enjoy your movie, you must let it play!"

You see, if you are to truly become empowered, you must allow yourself the opportunity to play out the masterpiece that is *YOUR LIFE.* Haven't you lived long enough in your comfort box of still limitations, both your own and others'? Allow yourself the freedom to breathe and be you. You are unique. You are a miraculous masterpiece, and you have all it takes. You have your beautiful life-movie to make and you are good enough to make it. Take ownership, be the director of your own movie and pay attention. It's time, and we are here to support you and keep you on track. Remember, WE *Summit Together!*

You are Enough
by Niamh Duffy

Feeling Good Enough

Have you ever felt you weren't good enough? I'm guessing that like me, at some stage in your life you felt that you weren't. There is a myriad of ways in which we can feel we are not good enough; a relationship break-up, feeling underappreciated in work. Maybe you're the last one in your peer group to find love? Do you feel you're not worthy of love? Maybe you don't try new things for fear of failure. Do you constantly compare yourself or aspects of your life to other people's, even down to the simplest of things like how you make a cake or the time it takes you to run a race? These are just a small set of examples out of countless ways that can make us feel like we don't somehow measure up to this perception of *"being good enough"*. Every one of us has experienced this feeling. It is a feeling or a mindset that has massive potential to lead us to some very unhappy places, but when we learn how to deal with it, we can feel so empowered and ultimately feel the happiness we deserve.

I am happy to share that I am good enough! Right now, in this moment, warts and all! Who am I good enough for? Me! Who else do I need to be good enough for? Nobody! It took me a long time to get to this mindset, there was a lot of wading through the old junk files of the brain and pressing delete, delete, delete! Like most things, getting here is one thing, staying here takes conscious effort on my part. Old habits die hard, and so cultivating a new set of beliefs takes daily awareness. My

intention in this chapter is to share with you some of the tools that helped me to change my own negative self-image, in the hopes that they might also help you to begin to realise that you too are enough, right now, in in this moment, warts and all! Let's start with an area that turned out to be a big one for me, validation!

Validation

One of the ways in which I was able to improve my self-worth was when I recognised that I had an outer need for validation. Validation is recognition that your feelings, actions or opinions are worthwhile. From the very day we become responsive human beings, we quickly learn that certain things we do will create a positive response in those around us. It begins with our parents clapping for us every time we learn to do anything new, from sitting up to crawling and even using the toilet for the first time. Our actions are rewarded with love, smiling faces and fanfares of applause. We learn to attach positive feelings to this obvious approval and strive to attain more of it.

As we leave the nest and enter the world of school, we are then rewarded by our teachers for completing our work in a timely manner, for being neat and well behaved. Recognition of a job well done spurs us on to seek more of the same. This kind of outer validation can be found not only in school but in all aspects of our young lives such as sports or dance groups or any organisations we attend, and it is a necessary part of learning for us as children. There are precious few children born with the emotional capacity to need only to believe in themselves to develop into confident self-loving adults. The majority of us as children measure our self-worth on the verification of those around us. I know for sure that I did, I needed to hear the words from someone else to feel like I was good at what I was doing.

But where this becomes a problem is when we, as mature adults, continue to need that outer validation from others, and fail to acknowledge the importance of our own self-worth. There comes a point in our lives where we must make the transition from seeking validation from others to telling ourselves and believing that *we are enough*, without needing to hear it from anybody else. The key to this, I believe, lies in becoming aware of whether you have made this transition or not and switching your mind-set accordingly. And if reading this you realise that you never received any validation as a child, you can take control and start now to validate yourself.

I hadn't been aware that I had not made the transition until well into my adult life. Throughout my adult work-life I had almost always been openly appreciated and rewarded for my efforts, purely because I chose to stay within comfort zones where I knew that praise would be given, thus satisfying my need for outer validation. In hindsight, this led me into a false sense of reality. To go from always having my work appraised, much like a child in school, to suddenly not, was quite a shock to the system. I took it as a personal attack on my skills and abilities. There was nobody patting me on the back saying "Well done" anymore. Since I had always attached outer validation to a job well done, I didn't ever think or realise that I could find that validation within. And so, in this one particular job I began to feel worthless and underappreciated. I went straight from school into work, and so with no other qualifications, I defined my self-worth on my efficiency in the workplace, but now with no positive feedback I suddenly felt a little bereft. We all want to feel valued in our place of work, or in any aspect of our lives for that matter, but when that is not a given, we must be content to know intrinsically that we are enough, but because I hadn't yet made the transition from outer to self-validation, I slipped into depression. My self-esteem fell so low that I had to take time away from work to regroup. I considered leaving the post but some part of me felt that, if I left, I would be missing out on an important life lesson, and in order to grow and become a stronger person, I needed to find out what that lesson was. I found the answer through counselling. I discovered that the real problem was not that I wasn't good enough, but that I had never *told myself* that I was good enough. I had gone through life believing that I wasn't enough, unless someone told me I was. Once I started to process this vital piece of information, things began to change. It was a light bulb moment. I asked myself, 'Since when did my self-worth depend on someone else's opinion or approval of me?' I was almost annoyed at myself for missing out on this simple fact for so long. I found the answer, as we usually do, in a memory from my childhood.

I have loved to sing for as long as I can remember. I was involved in a drama group where I excelled and yet I wasn't chosen for the school choir. I wasn't "good enough" to make the cut. I was crushed, and it really knocked my confidence as a singer. Despite the knock back, I continued to sing, but part of me felt like a fraud. I lacked true confidence. There was a feeling inside me that I had more to give as a singer, but something was holding me back. I could never accept a compliment because I never fully believed I was any good. I then read a book called *You Can Heal Your Life* by Louise Hay. It was while doing some work in relation to healing the inner child that the choir mistress popped into my head again and something clicked. Unbeknownst to myself I had held on to her rejection of me. I still held the view that I wasn't good enough for her, and so I wasn't good enough for me. That view stuck in my psyche all these years until I recognised that it was holding me back and then, through the eyes of an adult, I made the conscious decision to throw it out. I thought of her very clearly in my head and said with all the certainty I could muster "I don't need your approval anymore!"

I found a new confidence in myself. It was such a freeing feeling to know that I could delete that programme from my mind and start again. It was also such a simple thing that was holding me back that I really shouldn't have let someone have so much power over me. This new-found confidence rolled over into many other areas of my life, creating a domino effect of positive changes. I started to look at other areas where I had let someone else's opinion stop me from reaching my true potential and set about releasing those programmes too.

Growing up I'm sure we all at some point experienced teachers, group leaders or even loving family members who have either deliberately or more likely, completely inadvertently, knocked us back through their words or actions, things they may have said or done that stuck to us like glue, shaping our opinion of ourselves right into adulthood. However, the wonderful thing about emotional maturity is that we can now choose to make a conscious decision to completely park those negative views and start again with a clean slate.

Perhaps you can recognise that you have a need to be validated in order to feel good enough, maybe you can remember something someone once said to you that shattered your confidence and has held you back for too long. Ask yourself if you want to continue to let other people have a say in your self-worth or if you want to take control of it with your own self-validation and self-approval.

As I continued to work on improving some of my old patterns, I discovered something else that I hadn't been consciously aware I was doing, which was comparing myself to others.

Comparing Yourself to Others

Hands up if you've ever wished for another person's body? Have you ever wished for someone else's car, house, job or money?

Have you been envious of someone's achievements or talents? Whatever it is, we've all been guilty of it, either consciously or unconsciously. We've looked through the lens of other people's lives and came away feeling inadequate in our own. We could be talking about the lavish lifestyles of the rich and famous, a sibling or family member, or even the person who sits next to you in work. Comparisons can happen anywhere and with anybody.

For years I have been guilty of making comparisons in many areas of my life, and I didn't realise quite how much I was doing it until recently. I'm sure it began unconsciously when I was a child. Growing up as one of eight children, competition and comparison can be par for the course. Although you don't have to come from a big family to make comparisons, I see my two children comparing school reports every summer!

It has never been easier for us to compare ourselves to others. In the recent past, where people lived relatively private lives, the only comparisons we could make to others were based on what we could see through our windows into our neighbours' gardens. But now we live in a time where social media sites that connect us all and the little computers we carry around in our pockets that afford us twenty-four-hour access to these sites, we can see straight through the windows and directly into every aspect of people's lives. We know when they go to the gym, what they eat for breakfast, what clothes they purchase, all the places they visit, what achievements they and their children are clocking up etc. And while we click the "like" buttons to show our approval, it isn't beyond the realms of possibility that we then begin to compare our lives with the lives of those we are connected to, wondering if we are measuring up to the rest of society. 'Should I be working out more? Should I be going more interesting places? Should I be eating like that?' But in doing so, we prevent ourselves from being satisfied with who we really are and the life we are leading. Comparisons can lead us to feelings of inadequacy and can stop us from having confidence in ourselves. We all have a different path to take and we all have very different qualities to offer the world so, in order to be content in that, we shouldn't look at the actions of others to see if what we are doing is good or right or enough.

Of the many ways in which I discovered I was comparing my life to others, one such way was education. As I mentioned earlier, I didn't spend much time in college after school. I attended third level, where I was studying Communication and Media Studies, for a very short time. I left because of a bad review of my first real written assignment. It was returned to me decorated nicely with my tutors red pen which scared me because I thought I did a good job and it was the best I could offer with the knowledge I had at that time. I wasn't ready for the expectations of college tutors. College is a different ball game to school; you're very much expected to get by on your own. I was used to being lauded for my efforts in school, but college was the real world. There was no comfort zone here, no sugar coating, and at seventeen I just wasn't ready for that yet. I wanted my comfort zone again, so I left college, I got a comfortable office job and forgot about college completely for the next decade or so. I had my sights set on getting married and building a house and a good steady wage was far more conducive to that than four years of being a poor student.

It wasn't until the mortgage was secured, the wedding band was donned, and my two children had gained some level of independence from me that the idea of college returned. But it wasn't because I had found my calling, or that there was something I was desperately interested in doing, it was because I started making comparisons with other people. It seemed while I was happily playing house for the past twelve years, everyone around me was either finished or had gone back to education, earning degrees and advanced degrees.

I started to feel like the only person without the obligatory cap, gown and scroll photo for the mantelpiece and I felt very inadequate without it. Would having a diploma make me feel like part of the group? Would it be proof to the outside world that I had worth? Would it convince those around me who placed such a high value on education that I too was intelligent enough? I thought that if I had a degree, all these questions would be answered. I was judging my self-worth on the opinions of other people. I was judging my self-worth on the possession of a certificate, and completely disregarding everything else I had achieved in my life to date. I put no value on the work promotions I had achieved, on self-building a house or raising two children.

I thought having a degree would be the thing that would make me feel validated. It wasn't until someone pointed it out to me that I realised that the only reason I was looking to further my education at that time, was not for my benefit but to try and convince others that I was worth something, because I wasn't seeing it in myself. The person in question asked, "Why do you want a degree?" and I had no other answer only the one that came blurting out of my mouth, which was, "because then I'll be good enough!" She asked me, "Good enough for who?" This is such a good question to ask of yourself. Think about it, who are you trying to please? There is no board of directors sitting in some headquarters scrolling through images of the world's population deciding if people are good enough or not.

The fact is, I was good enough without a degree, I just didn't see it. It's not some piece of paper, or a certain job or the way you look or the amount of money you have that makes you good enough; you are good enough as you are! No outer force can change that in any way. And while I didn't quite believe this at first, it resonated with me through the days that followed. I kept telling myself "You are good enough" and I started to really believe it. And like the transition I talked about earlier concerning validation, I then started to believe that it didn't matter what education I had. I had major life experiences that qualified me and that I could be proud of. I decided that, if, and when I did decide to go back to college, it would be because I wanted to, not to prove myself to anybody, and once again I felt that sense of freedom. Something I had been carrying around like a weight on my shoulders was lifted! But now I had something more pressing to figure out.

Purpose

Everybody has a purpose. We are all born uniquely special individuals with a uniquely special purpose. Some people are lucky enough to discover their purpose very early in life, (how I envy those people!). Finding your purpose isn't always straight forward, as I know only too well. Doing what we love gives us a feeling that our life has worth and makes each day something to be grateful for, something to look forward to and can provide greater overall personal health and happiness.

I have discovered that finding my purpose and the key to my happiness didn't necessarily mean finding the right job, it was just about finding the right pastime. While it is some people's destiny to live their purpose through their daily work, you can find your purpose in anything that brings you joy and gives you a reason to get up in the morning, be it a pastime or through projects unrelated to your job.

I have been actively seeking my purpose for as long as I can remember. As a child I had trouble answering the question "What do you want to be when you grow up?" Of all the things I thought I might like to be, most interestingly perhaps was the idea that I wanted to be "a lady in a suit and high heels who travels by plane carrying a briefcase". I don't know what that job was, but it had a certain glamourous appeal to me. I could never fully answer the question until I had a significant amount of life experience under my belt!

Throughout my late teens and early twenties, I dabbled in various areas, hoping I might just find something that would ignite that spark that would keep the fire burning inside of me for the rest of my life. I felt like I was constantly being prompted to try certain things. For instance, I discovered Reiki in my early twenties and instantly felt a desire to learn as much as I could about the practice. I bought many books on the subject and in one they recommended becoming familiar with human anatomy, in order to best understand the practice. That led me to enrol in an Anatomy and Physiology class, which connected me with a Holistic Massage course. My intention was to become a massage therapist and course facilitator in the field of self-help and self-improvement. I began a small massage practice, which ultimately fizzled out when I discovered it wasn't bringing me as much joy as I thought it would. It wasn't my true purpose.

I carried on in this way for many years, trying things and not really feeling like I was getting any closer to the answer. In January 2018 I made a very conscious decision to commit to finding my purpose. The question I asked myself was "What are you really passionate about?" I forced myself to think hard, but the answer wasn't coming. Surely it should be easier than this to figure out? So, I decided to dig a little deeper. When I listen to people who have found their purpose, many of them say "I have always wanted to do this since I was a child".

So, I asked myself what were the things that I really loved to do as a child, and then it hit me, books! I loved reading, libraries, and bookshops as a child and I still do. I spent most of my childhood reading anything I could get my hands on, from Roald Dahl to John Grisham. All my pocket money and babysitting money went on buying new books. I had been writing for fun since I was a child. I remember once making a little tiny book about my life, all eight years of it. My sister said, "Someday we'll be reading your memoirs!"

A seed was planted that day, but never truly nurtured because I could never believe that I had the ability to write like the writers who had inspired me and brought me such happiness. I didn't have what it took, I wasn't good enough, even though without realising it I was always writing. I kept a diary for most of my teenage years and spent my days both in and out of school avoiding homework by writing letters to my friends, pages and pages of escapism, of creativity, humour and fun. Putting pen to paper has always brought me joy. Through bouts of depression, keeping a journal helped me release thoughts and feelings from my overcrowded head. When my children experienced illness as babies, writing my feelings was a form of therapy, a coping mechanism for my worries and anxieties.

Since making the decision that I am good enough as I am, the thought of writing isn't as unattainable as it once seemed, because I realised that I don't have to be a bestselling author to be happy as a writer, and that takes all the pressure away. I'm happy doing it even if I am the only one who reads it because it makes me feel good and satisfies my need to express my creativity and that's all that matters. I think sometimes we can put undue pressure on ourselves to think of a career that's going to bring us happiness, while also putting food on the table. It is possible to separate the two, pay the bills and satisfy your purpose on your own time. If your purpose eventually leads to a career, then think of it as a bonus!

Your childhood is a wonderful place to start, if you are stuck in finding a purpose. Think back to what gave you joy as a child, you might be lucky enough to stumble on something that you can rekindle in your adult life. Perhaps you felt happiest when in nature, or when swimming in the sea. Maybe you loved to build things, or to take things apart to see how they worked. You might have loved being in the company of animals. Rekindle your childhood passions and the happiness you seek may find you.

Getting it Right

We put so much unnecessary pressure on ourselves to get things right the first time because we are afraid that if it doesn't go right, we will be seen as a failure, which feeds into this idea that we are not enough. Only you get to decide if events in your life are failures, nobody else can make that judgement, and thinking anything otherwise is choosing to give other people power over your life and your decisions. Failure is just another word for learning, and if we are learning from all experiences, both good and bad then we are growing.

Are you a failure because you attempted to run a marathon and had to bow out six miles before the finish, or are you a success because you ran twenty miles and outran every spectator on the side-lines? Are you a failure for realising your dream of opening your own small business only to be forced to fold five years later because of a recession, or are you a success for taking those first steps to even try? Every perceived failure is an opportunity to learn, to try again. When Thomas Edison was asked how it felt to fail 1,000 times at making the light bulb he answered "I didn't fail 1,000 times. The light bulb was an invention with 1,000 steps". I love this statement, because it takes away that pressure of having to get something right the first time.

I used to worry so much about "what will people think" because I was so concerned about how others would perceive me. What would people say, if I failed? In my very large family, everybody passed their driving test on the first attempt. As next in line for the test, I felt immense pressure to keep the statistics up. I was a competent driver but got myself into such a state over having to pass first time that nerves took over and I failed miserably. I applied again and failed again. I told myself I had to pass this time and in placing unnecessary pressure on myself once again I was taken over by nerves. I applied a third time and before I took the test my husband gave me some great advice. He said. "Stop telling yourself you have to pass. Give yourself ten attempts to take this test, and if you pass before ten it's a bonus. If you don't, give yourself another ten attempts and keep doing that until you get it." And so, before I sat in the car, I decided that whatever the outcome, it didn't matter because I still had another seven attempts to go. In taking away the pressure to pass, I passed with flying colours on the third attempt! Not only did I take away the pressure of having to pass, I also decided not to care what other people thought of the result. Just because someone else succeeds first time doesn't mean you have to.

I often feel for young students when Junior and Leaving Certificate results are issued. The expectation and pressure on these children to achieve high grades for the masses of people who feel they have a right to ask, "How did he do"? This is fine, if the child gets a row of A's, but what if they don't do so well? Does anybody have the right to ask, let alone judge the results? Is it any of their business? This can be applied to anything in your life. Your life and the events that occur are your business alone, and nobody has a right to judge or to comment on them.

Since deciding not to worry about other people's opinions, I have allowed myself to move out of my comfort zone and experiment with new things. I challenge myself now in ways I was afraid to do before. The fear of looking like a failure in the eyes of others no longer holds me back because the way I see it is, as long as I am trying, I am not a failure.

Remember, there is no failure, only feedback. Use every experience both good and bad to push you to greater things.

Putting Yourself Down

Can you imagine standing in front of a child and berating them with insults? "You're fat! You're ugly! You'll never succeed! You're too short! You're useless!" Whatever the insult may be, take your pick and imagine yourself spitting these words at a helpless child. What do you think that would do to a child's self-esteem? And yet there are those among us who appear to have no problem with looking at our reflection in a mirror or using this kind of negative self-talk to insult ourselves in the very same way every day. Why are we so hard on ourselves?

Before I changed my old patterns, I couldn't pass a mirror without turning sideways to see if I'd lost five pounds, since I looked in the same mirror an hour previous to that. Every time I looked at myself, I would say "I'm so fat", "I hate myself", "I wish I was skinny", "I hate my legs" "I hate the shape of my face", I hate, I hate, I hate. Every day I went through the same ritual of putting myself down and filling myself up with self-hate. I was never content or happy with myself.

A lot of my opinions of myself were based on other peoples' judgements and comments that were lodged in my brain from way back in my childhood and truly served no purpose to me as an adult. There was the guy who alerted me to the fact that I had "fat legs", which up until that point I had been blissfully unaware of the size of any particular part of my body. After he expressed his opinion to me as an insecure teenager, it became the opinion I held of myself for many years to follow. Then there was my friend's brother who always gushed to me about how all his friends thought his sister was the best-looking girl in town because she was so gorgeous and everyone fancied her, which I took to mean that I wasn't all those things. And as previously discussed, the choir mistress who decided I didn't have what it took to be in the choir. I didn't have the emotional intelligence to allow these comments to pass over me as an impressionable teen and so I held them tight all through my life, quite unaware that I was doing so until I read a book called *You Can Heal Your Life*. Through the teachings in that book I began to see myself as a small child and I was able to recognise feelings and opinions that had negatively shaped me but no longer served me. I could then start the process of completely releasing them from my mind. I would imagine myself as an innocent little child every time I looked in the mirror. I couldn't look at that little child and say, "You're fat, you're ugly or you're weak." Instead I began to feel pain for that child, deep heart-breaking pain. I began to feel guilty for constantly putting her down, and since I'm being completely honest here, there were times when I sat looking in the mirror just crying for being so unnecessarily hard on myself for so many years. Self-confidence, as the very term suggests, begins with the self. If you can look in the mirror and say, "I hate myself", what kind of message are you conveying not only to yourself but to the rest of the world? If confronted with yourself as a child, if you were literally standing face to face with yourself as a child, could you bare to look him or her in the eye and say, "I hate you?" Well I discovered that I couldn't, and I no longer do. I've drastically changed my mirror-talk and my self-talk. For example, instead of looking at myself every day and saying, "I'm fat", I say "I'm happy with how I look, and I feel good about myself". If I've had a good day, or even if I haven't, but particularly if I have, I will look in the mirror and say, "I'm proud of you today, well done". There are enough people in the world willing to take us down, so why not raise ourselves up?

I urge you to start a daily self-love practice, and I don't mean conceited love, I mean beginning to create a habit of loving yourself for the person you are right now, without wishing to alter any aspect of your life in order to feel enough. You can do this through a daily journal where you might write the things you like about yourself or the things you did well that day. Or, do as I did and practice mirror work. Depending on where you currently are within yourself, this could be a more difficult task for some than others. In the beginning you may find it uncomfortable to even make eye contact with yourself in the mirror, but with regular practice it gets a lot easier. If you do find this exercise difficult, do what I did and fake it 'til you make it! Keep telling yourself how much you love yourself and how proud you are of yourself until you start to believe it, and eventually, you will start to believe it. Has doing the opposite of this got you any better results up to now? No? Well then, what have you got to lose?

Start today to at least notice how you speak to yourself either in your head or whenever you pass a mirror. Start to consciously listen to your self-talk and take note of whether you are building yourself up or tearing yourself down. You may be surprised at the amount of unconscious negative messages you are giving yourself. And always remember your inner child who needs to hear positive messages in order to grow stronger!

It's OK!
by Jennifer Clarke

For most of my life I was always in control. Well, I suppose that's how I saw it. I planned pretty much everything that could be planned, from the everyday things to big future goals. From an early age, I suppose I was that good kid in school and at home. I did well at exams both in school and college and I got a good job and continued on a decent path ever since. By nature, I was a left brain, logical thinker. I didn't really rely on or use my intuition. If I had a feeling about something, I would look for the logic to back the feeling up. I wasn't an impulsive person. I was used to structure and routine. I was very happy in this space, even right up until I married the man of my dreams in 2004, everything was planned to within an inch of its life. I have been called a control freak on many occasions. Probably a correct assessment!

I was however a good listener and that led to me becoming the 'counsellor' among my friends and colleagues. I was the girl that people came to with problems and I listened sympathetically and offered advice. I didn't however disclose my problems to many people, so I suppose I usually came across as the girl who seemed to have her life together.

I was a rule abider, well mostly, and as my husband and I started our new chapter as a married couple, we were supposed to conform to society, right? I had assumed that when we got married, I would just get pregnant or have a baby in our arms within one year. I was a thirty something year old and was essentially healthy. My friends of similar age were getting married and happily having babies, but for some reason, this did not happen for me. There was a constant question swirling in my head, 'How can this be happening to me?'. Having studied science in college and working in the Pharmaceutical industry, I looked at it like a science project, a problem to be solved. And off I went seeking the solution in many different places such as books, listening to others with children for little nuggets of information, internet forums etc.

After two years of marriage, I hadn't found the solution and there was still no baby. We had decided to give it two years. I did have a lot of information on how my body worked, I'm a scientist, I was gathering data! I knew my body inside out. I could have gotten a thesis out of all the information. At this stage, I knew there was something up, so I went to the GP. The logic wasn't matching up with the data and I had a gut feeling that something wasn't right. A rare occasion where my gut feeling was stronger than the facts. I had felt somewhat of a failure going to the GP as I, a control freak, had to ask for help, something I wasn't very comfortable doing. He had suggested that there was a possibility that on this occasion I may have had a very early miscarriage and with the facts I had presented, I may have had others too and just never realised. I had never had the joy of seeing a positive pregnancy test. So, the GP referred me to a gynaecologist. After some tests and exploratory keyhole surgery, it was confirmed that I had a condition called endometriosis where the endometrial tissue grows outside the womb causing pelvic pain. Receiving this information had both a positive and negative affect on me. On the one hand I was gutted that I had this incurable condition that could only be "managed" and becoming pregnant actually put the condition into remission - the irony of it! However, for the most part, I was happy that one, it was me who had the problem and not my husband as that meant I could take this on as a project and try and figure out the solution; and two, there was a known solid reason for not being able to have to a baby.

To help my endometriosis, the gynaecologist carried out some laser treatment to essentially "clean me up". I clearly remember the doctor telling me that even though the laser treatment was a success, endometriosis was here to stay. He told me that I now had up to a two-year window to try and get pregnant before the endometrial tissue built back up again. So, I planned ahead, as per the doctor's instruction.

Now as a control freak, this just added fuel to the fire for me. I already had a biological clock ticking away very loudly and now I perceived this news or pressure as another clock, a medical clock ticking over my head. However, this one was even louder.

During these two years I was still trying to solve my problem and work on my project. There was a new section added to my already growing collection of books and that was anything to do with endometriosis. I had many books on what you should and shouldn't eat having this condition which eventually got very confusing as in one book I could eat certain foods whereas, in another book I couldn't eat those foods. It was just exhausting!

Unfortunately, the two years flew by and absolutely nothing happened. No pregnancy, no baby. Soul destroying. And now family members, my friends, colleagues at work, had moved on to baby number two and baby number three.

My perfectly planned path forward was turning into a lot of dead ends. Sometimes with no visible way out. I couldn't control everything. This was very unsettling and something I found very hard to deal with. The only way that I thought I could claw any sense of control back was in having my little mini projects going on in the background while my otherwise normal life just went on. This took up another year and included me appearing to the world as this cool, calm and collect person, however in reality I was heartbroken and so sad on the inside.

Full steam ahead with project managing. It was very clear that the "obvious way" of becoming pregnant was not working. I had read many books on numerous subjects but that didn't lead to my happy ending. I came upon the *Billings Method*. Apparently, this was the way fertility was checked in the "olden days". It's a simple method of natural family planning. It is still used today by some, I believe. This also led to me getting to know my body very well!

I saw an advertisement for a fertility acupuncturist in my local area, so I booked an appointment. I had many needles placed all over my body and I got to relax for an hour which was a new phenomenon for me. It turns out that there was a positive here to having endometriosis. I would be in dreadful pain every month without fail so I managed to build up a high threshold for pain. My acupuncturist loved me coming into her clinic as she got to put needles into my feet, and I wouldn't flinch whereas most people find having needles placed into their feet quite painful. Yay for Endo!

My acupuncturist asked me to track my temperature. I was handed a graph and told that upon waking every morning I was to take my temperature and pencil the reading onto the graph. Honestly, I was delighted with the homework, it gave me something to focus on. The best part was that the acupuncturist's graph had a starting point of 35.8°C and my normal temperature was below this. I then got to make my own graph on my computer with loads of fancy graphics to go along with the results. I was graphing around 35.4°C to 35.9°C. Yes, I was freezing cold most of the time. It might explain while during the summer I would walk around in jeans and jumpers and everyone else would be wearing shorts and t-shirts! My poor husband also put in extra big radiators into all the rooms in our house to accommodate my freezing cold tendencies. In my head I was thinking that I might just have an inhospitable womb – just too damn cold for a baby to be happy to grow. So, I had a heating lamp placed over my tummy area, while I relaxed full of needles on the acupuncturist's bed. This felt like I was doing something positive. I was taking back the control in a manner.

I did always feel though that I couldn't let my guard down, when it came to searching for the solution to get me to that successful outcome of having a baby. So, I was on high alert most of time. I remember being in work one day and I was attending the scheduled 9am morning meeting which was held in an open plan office. I arrived a little early and I happened upon a vacant chair and sat down. One of the supervisors from the area came in and very sternly stated, 'Jesus woman, don't sit there!'. I jumped out of the seat and for a moment thought it was the chair that the Managing Director sat in. I asked, 'why not?'. And my colleague firmly stated, 'if you sit there, you will become pregnant!'. Wow! Really? He then went on to tell me that all the women who had sat in that chair at that desk were either on maternity leave or currently pregnant.

My mind was in overload. When he told me that story, I decided to believe that maybe the chair had magical powers! What if I was to seek out that chair every day for the 9am meeting and just see if the chair had any magical power. I was desperate OK! I was willing to give it a go. The plan was in place and was going well until one day I arrived and someone else was in the chair. I ended up faking a back ache to get him out of the chair. I know, desperate measures! Turns out that the chair didn't have magical powers after all.

Still no baby. It's getting harder now to keep up this so-called strong exterior. I feel like I am running out of time. I'm just so devastated.

Over these five years or so, there were days where I felt like I was on the *Truman Show*. You know where the director is sitting in the control room and is saying cue the heavily pregnant lady walking down the road and cue the new mammy with the new shiny buggy and brand-new baby. No matter where I went, I was surrounded by pregnant women, new mammy, babies and toddlers. They were everywhere.

I remember getting on a plane from Denmark with my colleague. We were seated at the top of the plane and the middle seat of the trio was free. During the flight a three-year-old kid walked down and climbed up onto the vacant seat and just sat there. She was a beautiful child, black shiny bobbed hair with a huge smile.

I can still see her face all these years later. Her dad came up to us and asked if she was bothering us. We said 'No, of course not!' So, he turned on his heel and walked back to his seat. My colleague and I just looked at each other in silence! I was horrified! Maybe the dad was happy to have a break from a busy three-year-old and my colleague and I looked pretty normal. Priceless! My colleague took out some paper and pulled out the tray for the child and I jumped in and gave her some pens. She doodled for a little bit and then said something in Danish and toddled off back to her dad.

As we sat there and interacted with this child, I was silently overcome with grief. It was a realisation to me at the time that this might never happen for me. I didn't show it on my face, well I don't think I did. I was getting quite good at hiding my emotional state and putting a smile on my face.

Now that I look back, I think my colleague knew there was something up with me as he made jokes about the situation saying things like, 'Bloody hell, we went on a training course to Denmark and came back with a child! What are people going to say?!'. I think he was just being kind and lightening the mood.

There was another time I remember where I experienced a very rough day. I believe I had a miscarriage, I had a similar experience to the one I had when I went to the GP previously. As usual, I would just get on with it and pick myself up and carry on as if nothing was wrong. I went to the local shopping centre, as I had decided that I was going to buy myself a new pair of shoes to try and make myself feel better. I remember meeting an old dear that I knew. We were all chat and then the stream of questions and statements began;

'So how long are you married now?'.

'Five years! You wouldn't what to leave it much longer to have a baby as you aren't getting any younger'.

'God love that poor husband of yours'.

'I know you are one of those career women, but you are going to regret it'.

'You need to have a child, as who is going to look after you when you get old?'.

And then off she went with not a notion of what she had left behind. I was already a wreck that day, but this just destroyed me. It was then I became convinced that there had to be a club whereby you reach a certain age and they hand you a licence which allows you to ask the most inappropriate questions at the most inappropriate times in a very public place.

I believe that most of my friends knew that there was something going on with me, but it wasn't something that we really spoke about. When they told me that they were pregnant, I could tell that they had struggled telling me as they didn't want to hurt me especially when they were pregnant on number three and I hadn't had number one! Each and every announcement had a profound effect on me. Depending on how I was on any particular day, and how the announcement was made, I would go through so many emotions. I would feel so sad that it would feel like I'd been hit by a bus. I would feel so jealous enough to take my breath away. I would feel so angry as this would serve as another reminder that although I was doing all the right things to achieve a successful pregnancy, my friends appeared to be getting pregnant so easily. I would feel so sorry for my husband. I would be going home again to tell him that someone else we knew was pregnant. This was another reminder that we were getting closer to "Childless Ville". This is just how I saw it.

In fairness, I always felt genuinely happy for my friends when they told me as I do believe pregnancy is an absolute miracle. Even if I was heartbroken for many personal reasons, they were my friends after all. But the guilt would slide in when the negative emotions would pop up. I questioned why I could feel this bad, after what was nothing but an amazing moment for my friend. How could I feel any negative emotion in this situation?

I was experiencing very negative feelings that seemed to go against the grain for me. I found it difficult to deal with these and at the end of some days I would just feel like a failure. This was something that I couldn't sit an exam for, or hand in an assignment. I didn't know what to do. My world on the outside was a very busy one and appeared to be successful, but on the inside, I just felt so sad. I was the queen at hiding how I felt on the inside but there were cracks showing.

I had many coping strategies. If I was on a night out and I knew that I was going to meet someone that had already announced their pregnancy, I would set myself up for an easy exit. I would go over to the person and congratulate them, ask them a few customary questions and if things started to get a bit rough for me, I would excuse myself saying I had left my drink behind and I'd see them later but then never return!

I even tried talking myself into believing that I didn't want a baby. The financial burden for ever more, the sleepless nights, no free time, the havoc it'll play on my marriage. The list went on. But still I never believed any of it and I couldn't convince myself of it either.

During this journey I found that there were things that I had chosen to give up, one being a positive mindset. I spent a lot of time in my head in "Negativity Land", as a result of not being able to become pregnant. I saw it as a big failure and my fault. By constantly trying to figure out how I would become pregnant, I missed out on just having fun. I wasn't present sometimes when I was out socialising with friends or family. Living in the moment and just going with the flow wasn't a space I was spending time in. I also lost some friends. Some had moved on along their journeys and that included kids for them. They were busy with their new additions and I sometimes found it difficult to be around new babies. It reminded me of my failure. It was very emotional for me with all these different emotions spinning around; sadness and anger because it wasn't happening for me, guilt and jealously because I felt bad for not being happy for my friend, shame because I couldn't give my husband a child. When I look back on this journey now, I was really tough on myself.

The pressure was just getting too much and one day I finally confided in a close friend and found out that she shared a similar story to me. I wasn't the only person in the world to be suffering with fertility issues. She had me consider the possibility of fertility treatment. I had heard this before from the GP and the gynaecologist, but if I am honest, I don't think I really listened to them. I made an appointment with my GP and he wrote a referral letter. We had a consultation and then underwent three IUIs but none of them were successful. I blamed the clinic for the failures. It was easier to do that. I couldn't take on the mental load of it being my fault. We changed to another clinic, a new hope. We met with the consultant and he talked to both of us and told us the do's and don'ts of the journey ahead of us.

I remember very clearly a surreal moment after this meeting with the consultant. He had basically said that we would go straight to IVF treatment and to just let them in the clinic do their job. Such a simple statement but for the first time I really believed him, and I just let go. It felt like I handed my body over to him and mentally said, 'It's all yours'.' I can't figure this out any more. I needed the expert help. It felt OK to do this. It was OK. The relief was huge. Logic was taken over by my intuition and this time, it felt right.

I was so mentally and emotionally exhausted at this time that I really needed to start looking after myself. I was about to undergo a gruelling process and I needed to be physically, emotionally and mentally prepared. There were also the financial aspects of the process. It's bloody expensive! I know people who have re-mortgaged their houses in order to "try again". We had already ready spent a few thousand on the IUIs. Were we going to get to that stage?

We went ahead with the IVF treatment and there really are not enough words to describe how gruelling it was. I remember my husband walking in from the Pharmacy and handing me these two big bags of medication. I just assumed they were for three IVF cycles, but in fact the medication was for just one treatment. I couldn't believe it!

One of the interesting things about the meds this time was that I didn't read any of the patient information leaflets (PIL). Up until then I read every PIL from start to finish even if it was just a simple painkiller. I just didn't want to know any of the side effects at all. I didn't want to add negatively to the process. I have done enough of that already. In hindsight, probably not the best thing to do.

With the treatment full steam ahead, it came to the day for egg harvesting. It is a very invasive procedure and the amount of hope wrapped up in that day is palpable. Fourteen eggs were harvested, twelve fertilised and by day five, four embryos were left. This is where you truly understand the meaning of quality over quantity. We just needed one quality embryo but getting those phone calls over the five days while the embryos are 'cooking' and hearing the numbers dwindle is not to be underestimated. That last phone call from the embryologist when she told us that there were four embryos left was so emotional. It was a Sunday afternoon and we were driving around when my phone rang. The embryologist is required to ask you a few standards questions to ensure the information is correct, name, date of birth, etc and that you are in fact the right person. It felt endless! Then she delivered the amazing news, there are four blastocysts remaining, two will be transferred tomorrow and two will be frozen. What a beautiful statement. There were lots of tears that day.

We had already agreed with the consultant that if there were two or more embryos on day five, two would be transferred. Transfer day is the easiest day in relation to all the other procedures I went through. It's simple and quick. I lay there for a while and the doctor came in to say that they were happy with how it had gone, and I could go home now. I hadn't factored in what was going to happen next. I now had to stand up. Wouldn't the blastocysts fall out? I knew how gravity worked! I was assured that they wouldn't, but I made my husband drive home very quickly so I could just get into bed and lie down. I was super paranoid! I had chosen to stay at home for the infamous two-week wait. In my head I needed to give this the best chance of working and this to me was the best thing I could do. I know some women prefer to get back into the rat race just to stay busy. They need the distraction. It's completely personal, so do what is right for you. I now just had to wait two weeks until I did a pregnancy test. Easy, right!!

I was scheduled to do the pregnancy test on Saturday 17th July 2010. It was the night before and I was sitting watching the television with my husband. At about 11.30pm and my husband asked if I was going to do the test. Being a scientist and a rule abider, there was no inkling in me to do the pregnancy test as it wasn't the correct time! In saying that the biggest part of me was clinging onto hope. I wanted to hold onto the hope for another half an hour. I was afraid that if I did the test and it was negative, the hope would disappear, and I would have the endure an extra half hour of devastation. I just wanted to hold onto the hope.

In the end I did the test at 11.50pm! I went upstairs to the bathroom and did the test, turned it over so I couldn't see the results window, came back down the stairs went over to my husband and he stood up, turned over the test and there was the most amazing sight I had ever seen, two beautiful blue lines!

I was absolutely hysterical! My poor husband didn't realise that two blue line meant I was pregnant. So, he didn't know! He couldn't tell if I was happy-hysterical or devastated-hysterical! He'd given up trying to figure that one out! He tried to calm me down. He held me, then got me to sit down on the couch. He then said, 'What is it?'. I eventually told him that we had finally done it! We were having a baby! Or should I say babies as it turns out! We were having twins.

Our beautiful boy/girl twins were born the following February and our new chapter in our lives began. Two became four.

Throughout this journey there is one thing that stands out for me and it is understanding the HOW versus the WHY. *How* was I going to become pregnant versus *Why* did I want to be a mother?

I spent years trying to look to the future and constantly analysing the HOW. How do I figure out how to become pregnant? I read so many books, I listened so intently when anyone, including friends and family, would talk about becoming pregnant or having babies and I tried to pull any useful nuggets of information from them in the hope that their piece of information would be all I needed to know to solve my problem. I went onto anonymous forums where people would post up their fertility issues on line and others would share their advice. I was constantly on the lookout for the 'how'.

I can safely say that I really wasn't living my life to the fullest at all. I had forgotten to have fun, terrified that I'd miss something important related to becoming pregnant. I forced myself to go to Christenings, even though I found them very tough to bare. I attended my friend's kid's birthday parties and I would "get a lend of" my niece and bring her along just so I wouldn't stand out, although, it probably made me stand out even more. I would even go above and beyond and buy a really decent present for the birthday boy or girl and totally embarrass the mother. I only realised this much later. I was over compensating, but I didn't know what else to do. I was constantly on edge and wasn't enjoying the journey. This had an impact on all my relationships. I never really relaxed into anything. I was on constant 'how' mode.

Looking back, there was an easier route that I could have taken and that was to only focus on the 'Why'. I believe that in a situation like this, where you need to be extremely invested, your 'why' must be big enough to make you cry. Mine was! I simply knew in every cell in my body that I wanted to be a mammy. Not being one was just too devastating for me to comprehend at the time. I think my 'why' helped get me through the really difficult times. I did have those conversations with myself where I would ask, 'What if this doesn't happen?' I would try and prepare myself but my 'why' was always there and it was routed deep down inside me.

This is something that I have used throughout my life since. I am a very logical and analytical thinker so using my gut, and feeling it, is somewhat of a new phenomenon. I always made decisions based on facts and figures. I believe that the gut feeling is like a knowing and an understanding of the 'why' in any situation. It is the feeling in your bones! If I am honest, I could probably use it more and I do revert to the facts and figures, which also serve me well. However, if I have the facts and I still don't know what my next steps are, I try and use my gut, my knowing, my why.

What also helped was coming to terms with being open to possible variations on how to achieve the 'why'. This means that you stop trying to force the 'how'. I have met many women that have achieved becoming a mammy but how they got there was very unexpected. Some ended up going down the donor route, some the adoption route, one woman was unsuccessful with various treatments however, changed her career to devote her life to children. There can be many ways to achieve your goal, you just have to be open to it.

For me the why is very much intertwined with hope. If you lose the hope there isn't much left to keep you going. Hope gets your through from one stage to the next. And this is true for all of life's trials and tribulations. Hope has such a positive feeling and helps with how you assess situations and helps you with your decisions.

My journey to this stage of my life has had many ups and downs and, as I look over the past few years, I realise how resilient I was. I think as human beings we don't stop often enough to truly take in what we do to get through our day. Some days are tough, and I have learned that it's OK. We just start the next day and hope for a better day. We are so resilient, and we should commend ourselves for that.

Both men & woman are very powerful human beings and we need to remind ourselves that sometimes when life throws us lemons, that we are just fantastic at making lemonade. We need to remind ourselves often that:

- It's OK to know that you are trying your best and that some days are just better than others.

- It's OK to give yourself a break and know that you did the best you could. It's OK to just learn from it.

- It is also OK to ask for help when you just can't do it alone anymore. It's not a failure.

- It's OK to learn from your mistakes. That's how you grow.

- It's OK to remind yourself how amazing you really are.

- It's OK to be the best version of you and shine your light.

- It's OK to just be you.

After everything I had been through and all the logical data I had stacked up, I had defied logic and I had let go and believed in the process and my intuition. I went on to give birth to a gorgeous little man, two years after my twins, with no intervention. Everything was OK

Overcoming Obstacles, Despite Limitations
This is ME

by Tracey McCann

Allow me to introduce myself, my name is Tracey. I am a thirty-year-old woman from Dublin, Ireland. I have achieved quite a lot so far within those thirty years; I am a bestselling author, international inspirational speaker, life coach and disabled advocate. I have travelled to many parts of the world with my partner, and I also speak up for the disabled. The reason I am, in my opinion, a voice for the voiceless, or a Disabled Advocate, is because despite my many wonderful achievements, I too have a physical disability. Also, despite the fact that I am a public speaker, one who has spoken in front of hundreds of people and received countless standing ovations for delivering my message, despite these facts, I cannot verbally communicate. Lastly, even though I am a bestselling author of a book that delivers such a strong and powerful message of hope and endurance, it was not that long ago that I felt like giving up and that all was hopeless. My name is Tracey, and this is my story.

When I was a child I really enjoyed going to school because, even from a young age, I acknowledged the importance of being part of society, and how vital it was to surround myself with my peers.

One day in particular however, my world changed forever. This day was the 16th of September 1996; I was eight years old and in second class. On that day I awoke as normal and proceeded in getting ready for a school trip to a *Playzone*. However, I was not feeling too good; it felt as though I was getting the beginning of a cold. I suffered a lot with my sinuses as a child and still do to this day, and so both my Mam and I just put it down to that. Mam was trying to keep the excitement up within me by reminding me how much I was looking forward to it, and how much I would enjoy it. When I arrived at the school with Mam, who was holding my hand walking up to my class, it was passed 9am. My Mam explained to my teacher that I was not feeling the best and to keep an eye on me. The teacher replied that she would and said to me that I would enjoy the day, it was better than remaining at home, and I smiled in agreeance. I let go of Mam's hand and went over to my best friend, all the while trying to calm myself, "Yes, it will be a good day". Suddenly, I got this strange feeling that something bad was about to happen, it was a truly horrible sensation. I remember looking back at Mam and feeling terrified in that moment. I did not understand what was causing this nervous discomfort. In the end however, I decided to go along on the school trip, despite how I felt at that time and later in the day as my apparent "sickness" worsened. While playing chase with the other children at the *Playzone*, I felt light headed and suddenly fell from a rope ladder, and from that moment until this one I have not been the same Tracey as before that faithful day.

Over the following few months I spent my days in the hospital, being prodded and poked at by Doctor's who just scratched their heads, as the condition of my body worsened. In the end, after months of drama and misdiagnoses, it was discovered that I had a genetic disorder known as Rapid On-Set Muscular Dystonia with Parkinsonism. From the moment I fell off that rope ladder I was in a constant, seemingly never ending, and excruciating spasm. To make matters worse, I had completely lost my ability to verbally communicate. I would spend the remainder of my childhood, teenage years, and early twenties, dealing with a different form of pain, the pain of loneliness, and the pain of not feeling that I have a purpose. I was physically and emotionally disabled.

Fast forward to present day, I am a strong-minded individual, who within the past few years especially, has a brilliant outlook and attitude towards life. I now look at the positive in all and any situation and try to focus intensely on what I can do and find solutions around what it is that I find difficult. Maintaining the knowledge of that old age saying, if there is a will, then there is a way. I also now know that anything is possible, with the right mindset and an equal measure of the right attitude.

While I acknowledge that we may not all have a disability per se, we are all disabled in one way, shape or form, by our obstacles. What we all must do on a daily basis is to firstly acknowledge our own limitations, and then actively find our own unique ways of dealing with these.

I am Tracey, I am unique, and *this is me.*

Celebrating YOUR uniqueness

I want you to honestly ask yourself, have you ever heard of Rapid On-Set Muscular Dystonia? I am going to assume that you have not, neither had my Mam and I. That was the most frustrating fact for us at the time. Dystonia was not commonly known, unless you were an expert in heredity neurological muscular disorders. Eventually, it began to become recognised that this was affecting a handful of families in this country, prior to that we assumed that we were alone. Even with that in mind, there are many various forms of Dystonia, and the form that I have is so rare that only five families in the world have it. This simple fact makes me unique. When I was in my mid-twenties I was informed by the doctors that there were different treatments recommended to treat four of the five different types of Dystonia, and all of these treatments were successful, I tried a number of these treatments which unfortunately did not work successfully for me, in fact I became worse while undergoing these treatments, this too makes me unique. I came to the realisation that I needed to use my own intuition, I needed to heal myself. I needed to embrace my uniqueness and feel proud of that as the fact that it was. I needed to think differently about my situation and celebrate that I have within myself the power to overcome the obstacles that life has given me. I must continuously work on improving myself, which I will succeed at doing with the right support. I have discovered my own way, through listening to my heart. My ability to overcome my life challenges also makes me unique, and I am proud to celebrate that.

To overcome our obstacles, we must come to the realisation that it is not the obstacles that define us; it is how we react and overcome those obstacles that give the outside world a true definition of our uniqueness. There are currently seven and a half billion people living on earth and with such a vast selection of individuals populating the planet the laws of probability states that there is likelihood that two or more of those individuals are exactly alike. Have you ever met someone who reminds you of someone you know, and that person lives on the other side on the world? The truth that we all must realise however is that nobody is the same, even identical twins are completely different, they can have different likes and dislikes, two completely different personalities and if you studied them intensely you would notice both their similarities, and their unique differences. Bearing all of this in mind, once we recognise that everyone is different, we can begin to recognise what it is that makes other individuals, and ourselves unique. Whether you have a physical or mental disability, if you have an ongoing health problem, you find it difficult to learn, or you struggle with your appearance, whatever issues you face daily about yourself my advice is this, acknowledge your pro's, work on what you have right now, learn new ways around doing things that you struggle with, connect with the right people, people who are going on a similar path as you, and lastly, know that you are not alone. Everyone is going through different journeys, defining their lives by choosing their own paths, and facing their obstacles in their own unique way. Despite any obstacles we face, and regardless as to how we face them, the most important thing we can do for ourselves is to learn to love everything about us, flaws and all, and to be proud of who we are as individuals. When we can celebrate the individual people we are, this can 'ground' us, and bring joy and clarity into our lives. We are all unique, *celebrate your own uniqueness.*

It's okay to be YOU

When I had finished in primary school, and the time arrived for me to make the transition into secondary I decided that I did not want to go to the same secondary school as my primary school friends. Instead I wanted the take a leap and make a fresh start, with new people from a completely different area. At the time, some people thought Mam and I were not being sensible with our decision to separate me from my friends who I had grown up with and who knew the Tracey before Dystonia. However, I felt in my heart that I needed a change of scenery, and a new challenge as I wanted to step out to the world on my own two feet and unsupported. I acknowledged that secondary school was a very important part of life for people, as it can shape the people that we become and is vital to our internal growth from a child, to a teenager and then to a young adult. In that moment I knew that I needed to make the right choice as this decision would define me for the remainder of my life; it had the potential to serve my highest good. When I had selected my secondary school, I was excited but naturally enough very nervous. By putting myself out there with no armour protecting me made me aware as to how vulnerable I was. I knew the road that I chose would not be easy, nor would I be welcomed fully. It was also extremely tough on the teachers in the school as they had no clue how to assist me in learning; I was the first disabled student to attend that school. It was a learning curve for everybody. It was a very daunting experience for me, and everybody concerned. The first three years were the most difficult as I honestly did not feel that I belonged, I was an outsider masquerading as if I was the same. Given the fact that I had a physical disability, which I was still coming to terms with, and needed an extra hand, and then add to the mix the fact that I cannot verbally communicate properly, and you can imagine how awkward I felt, I was very vulnerable during those early years of my schooling life.

Even though there were days when I wanted so badly to give up, I did not, I kept showing up. I did not realise at the time but in those tough moments that were really testing on me, I was becoming stronger and more in tune with myself. I became more confident and felt that I could break free from my negative mental situation created the day my Dystonia 'kicked in'. People began to see the real me, the real Tracey who is "mad" and has the ability to laugh her way through life, despite how negative a situation gets. I began to feel accepted and loved for who I was. I started to feel part of society and content. I woke up happy every day before going to school. Throughout that whole experience, I learned two things, firstly, the importance of sticking with something that you know will be beneficial to you in the long run, you will be tested again and again, but the benefit of sticking with it will make it worth it, trust me. The second and most important thing I learned is this, we all must embrace who we truly are, and love who we are. Realise that throughout any transitional periods within our lives, we all must become OK with being true to ourselves.

To you, the reader, I will say this, if you are presently struggling to find a solution to an obstacle that is holding you back the first thing you must do is be comfortable with yourself, and the decisions that you make along your journey. If you do not want to be the person that you presently are then do some soul searching and ask yourself what makes you happy. You will then discover who you are truly meant to be.

Know YOUR worth

When we were born, we all had the exact same human need, the need for safety, both physically and emotionally. It is due to this need that when we are faced with an obstacle that pushes outside of our comfort zone, we perceive this as danger, and as though it is outside of our 'safety zone'. It is easier, and 'safer', for us to just go along with crowd, and not take chances. We are just moulded into believing that the life we have now, is the life we will have for the remainder of our days, it is just the way our life as to be.

For a great number of years, I did not know why I was here; I constantly questioned why it was that at 8 years old I was given such a difficult challenge to overcome. I would constantly question all the negative situations in my life at that time, and then I would look for an answer to a question I asked myself repeatedly "Why am I depressed?"

Now I know that this is not the solution to overcoming ANY obstacle, self-pity will not get you results. We automatically get bad/negative conscious replies to those questions we ask ourselves daily. My advice to you all is this, take control of your thoughts, and say to yourself daily *"I might feel depressed at the moment, but I know that this moment will pass"*. Our thoughts control our emotions, which we require to be in a positive state in order to take positive action in overcoming whatever obstacles we face, in order to get positive results.

Honestly ask yourself, would you want someone else to be hit with your problems? That person probably would not be able to cope with them mentally and or physically. When faced with an obstacle, if you spend moments pondering to yourself "why me?" Here is what I will say to you, why not you. You have two choices when faced with an obstacle, you can either crumble in submission, and wallow in self-pity, or you can acknowledge that by overcoming this hurdle and facing this head on you will not only achieve, but you will learn, so choose to keep moving forward. For years I was full of similar questions, I was so low, full of anger, living in other people shoes, I felt weak, and useless. I was getting more angered at myself because I started to notice, and dislike, the negativity that swamped me. Nobody wanted to know me, well, not the type I wanted in my life anyway. Negative attracts negative. When I slowly took myself out of the 'bubble' that I had placed myself in I realised I did deserve happiness. The key to reaching this happiness was simply doing more of what made me happy, like going for a walk, being around the family dog, playing sports. I also had to do more of what challenged me on a daily basis, such as verbally communicating with others.

Unfortunately, I got Dystonia, but the more I focus on the negative side of it, the less positive changes will happen for me. However, by focusing on the positive, respecting my self-worth, working hard on myself, and developing my mental and physical state, I have improved greatly. I have done all of this because I wanted to, and I believed I deserved a brilliant life. I realised that I have so much to give; I can help so many people with and without disabilities. I can provide people with the tools required in not only facing an obstacle, but overcoming it, whatever their situation.

In my experience, if you want to have a great life then you have to be willing to stand out from the crowd and allow yourself to shine. Be heard and let people know you for all the right reasons. You can create a fantastic life for yourself, you can make it over that obstacle, and you can encourage and inspire others to do the same. Visualise your desired result, focus in the steps required, and most importantly, believe in your greatness, believe in your worth, and then go for it. You are WORTH it.

Whatever situation you find yourself in, repeat these words, believe in these words, "*I deserve a great life, because I am worthy of greatness*".

Recognising YOUR "limitations"

First and foremost, allow us to talk about the elephant in the room, none of us are perfect, we are all not without our own individual flaws and our own physical and or mental limitations. Being aware of that fact we can now move on to the second important thing worth noting, important due to it being unrealisable to many people today. These limitations we carry around with us like heavy excess baggage do not and should not define us. Now that that has been stated, this leads us to the obvious question, what are our own individual limitations? Are these limitations genuine e.g. a physical disability? Or are they something entirely different, a restriction that you have fabricated in your mind from listening to too many pessimistic people, or yourself even. Whatever your situation, I am here to tell you that your limitations do not control you, you can overcome them, you can find a way around them, and most importantly, you can choose, if you wish, to surpass them.

For me, the limitations that I face, and have faced since reluctantly, are obvious if you ever meet me in person. These limitations had prevented me for years from expressing myself verbally, which in turn made me feel so alone and isolated. I used to feel that I merely just existed, and as though I was just floating around not knowing how to communicate, and thus, how to socialise. I believe that for a large portion of my early years, it was not my disability that held me back, it was my inability to recognise my restrictions, adapt quick enough, and overcome those restrictions. If only I knew then, what I know now.

When we recognise our limitations, we will also become aware of the fact that we may require support in finding a way around, or even over, these limitations, even if this support is just to assist us in a small way, with overcoming an obstacle. Quite frankly, and in a lot of cases that I am aware of, if we do not have the required support and we are struggling, then it could take much longer for us, if we ever even do, to achieve a desired outcome. There is no shame, or harm committed by recognising that you MAY need assistance to get to where you want to go in your life, I know I have, and still do. Think of it this way, if one of the possibilities for you achieving a goal is to do something that potentially causes either yourself, or other people, to be placed in any sort of harm's way, and the only way for you to avoid this harm is to ask for assistance, then ask for assistance. I will admit that yes, I love to take risks, but only if I feel 100% safe in what I am doing and have the right support around me, if something does go wrong. This is not, despite how it may appear, a contradiction; this is called "boxing clever". I am a risk taker, but I only take calculated risks, I cover my bases just in case. If you want to achieve something that will make other people look at you in awe, and give you pride at what you have accomplished, then you too need to take calculated risks. That being said, I like living, and as such have no plans to do a forty-foot plunge off the edge of a cliff!

Life is made up of moments, and in some of these moments we are faced with obstacles, and we recognise our limitations. When we are in these moments, we have two choices, fight or flight. Do as I have done, choose to fight, and if you find that you may need help during this "battle", never ever be ashamed or afraid to ask for it. You are not alone; do not act as though you are.

Surpassing YOUR "limitations"

During the early years of my learning to adapt to this disability, the consultants were looking into communication aids to assist me with reintegrating myself back into society, verbally at least. However, when I heard, for the first time, these devices that could communicate whatever I inputted into them, I felt physically sick. I grew a fear around using these devices because it was not my voice, it was an American voice, and it sounded artificial. I could not, and did not, want to get my head around it. Looking back on it now, in retrospect, this was a huge limitation that I had at the time. I was looking for a way to communicate with other people, while being angry that I could not do this verbally myself, all the while I had a device that could get me over this massive hurdle, but I refused to use it because it made me more self-conscious of the fact that I could not manage without the assistance of an artificial voice.

As the years progressed, I learned that I had many sounds that I could make, but I could only use them around my close family. It took me years to use my actual voice, as it was very difficult to hear, and again, I did not like how it sounded. I would 'ball my eyes out' while lying in bed, looking up to ceiling saying to myself "I want my voice back, I miss it so much" I was devastated. Losing your ability to speak has such a massive impact on your life, more than you would realise. Your voice is personal to you, it is *unique*. Every person that hears this unique sound coming from your mouth gets a higher sense of the type of person you are and may even be able to gauge your emotional status somewhat, all from how you talk. I realised early on that I had to work that bit harder, for people to see the amazing person I am, and that under all of my pain of loss, there was brightness and a burning desire to make a difference. Developing myself over the years, through going to mainstream school, opening myself up to new experiences, learning self-gratitude from the progress that I was making and that I was living as the best version of myself, combined with my discovery that verbal communication is only 7% of the overall communication methods humans use, the other 93% is nonverbal. All the steps that I have made have not been easy, but then anything worth doing is never going to be easy is it? We are kidding ourselves if we think otherwise.

The progress that I have made within the past two years alone has been incredible. I have stepped out from the shadows of despair and loss that I had become somewhat accustom to. I now feel comfortable with myself and have learnt to love myself each day. *That is where real change starts*, that is where making the leap from struggling with a limitation, to surpassing a limitation happens. You must first love yourself, and all you have achieved and overcome so far. You must realise that whatever your current or future challenges are, you will face them head on, and you will win every time. *Anything is possible, once you believe in, and love yourself*. I have now come to terms with using that American robot voice that I put off using for so long, I finally want to be heard, and to be taken seriously. I took the decision to use it after so many years of resisting it because I realised that, just like my story, and my 'disability', this talking application that I now use at my events sets me apart from others in my field, and it gives me my own uniqueness.

Keep doing what you can do because your disadvantages give you your own unique limitations. What you must do is be unique enough to surpass those limitations, in whatever way you can.

How YOU should deal with Naysayers

When I was in my teens and early to mid-twenties I felt as though I was going around in circles. I felt depressed and frustrated with myself. All of this was due to not knowing what I was meant to do, and I felt like I was wasting my life. Obviously, I did not like that feeling, and I did not want to remain with it either, I would often find myself looking at everyone else's life and wishing mine was even just a tiny bit like theirs. I spent a large amount of time in my bedroom, looking out the window, watching the world fly by me. I knew that I needed to take back the control over this situation and create the happy life that I knew I deserved. As bad as this may seem, I felt that certain people were happy to leave me there in my own solitude once they knew where I was, and that I was 'safe'. Nobody would come near me or offer any assistance. The only true support I felt I received in those years was from my Mam and my Dad, Stephen. They would always talk to me, doing their best to get me to focus in on the idea that things will not always be like this, things will get better. I would have everything that I had spent years dreaming of during those times, looking out my window and visualising. Then, as they were leaving my fortress of 'solitude', they would always make an attempt at encouraging me to go out, while making it sound exciting and promising. All this support greatly helped me, but it was I who had to take that step out and join things myself and no longer become dependent on others, which I finally did. When we depend on others, we can become overly reliant on them, and this is never good. We can then, in turn, find it more difficult putting ourselves out there, as an independent individual. This can be a very daunting experience. Taking this step was tough for me. I was aware that my physical disability drew more attention to me, it is not everyday people come across someone who finds verbal communication difficult, unless they work directly with the disabled. That was something that I had to get over, and I did. I threw myself into everything that I could, drama, bootcamp, boxercise, all of which really put me out there. These improved my confidence rapidly.

During my time spent looking out the window, my biggest dream was to travel the world. To explore the different cultures, meet new people, and engulf myself in the sheer beauty of the world in which I was hiding away from. At the time I did not know how I would do this, but I always had an inner belief it WOULD happen. For some reason, I had an overwhelming desire to visit Australia. Maybe this was due to the distance, and to be able to say that I have been to the other side of the world. In my head, this sounded pretty amazing. When the opportunity came to me, I jumped on it head-first and booked it. I had asked my boyfriend, Patrick, if he would be interested and was delighted when his reply was yes. I used money that I had built up over the years and booked it. Patrick was shocked and amazed at my quick and positive action.

We had a whole year to plan everything, and nobody said anything to us during the majority of that year, they were just a bit taken back and acted happy. As soon as it got closer to our departure date however, some of them were saying to my Mam that she "can't let Tracey go", and that she "will have to go in and cancel it yourself", all without my permission. They wanted my Mam to sneak into town where I had booked it and cancel the trip on me. I know it was in great part due to their concern for my safety, but these same people did not want to know me when I was at my lowest, now all of a sudden, they felt the need to get involved when I was at my highest. I knew myself that I was well capable of doing this, I was with a good person who was an experienced travelled man. Both Patrick and I ignored all the pessimistic views of the naysayers, and went to Australia anyway, and we had a brilliant and safe time. *Nobody was stealing my dream from me.* I and I alone, know what I am truly capable of. When it comes to my dreams or goals, I listen to me and me alone, while considering my own safety, and the safety of my partner. I go through the process of the challenge ahead in my mind, focus in on what I have to do, and pay no attention to the negative, unless it is genuine good advice. Now that people realise that I am a responsible adult, they trust me, and wish me well on my travels.

My message to you all is this, listen to yourself, trust yourself, you are living your own life. If there is something that you really want to do, and you believe that you are capable, then do not listen to dream stealers, or naysayers. They may not always mean harm, but always be aware that *this is your life, not theirs*. Do what makes you happy, you are not here to appease the needs of others.

The importance of rewarding YOURSELF

When we were young, we actively sought out ways of being rewarded for even our tiniest accomplishments. However, as we developed into adults, some of us lost the notion of positive action equals positive reward. In my opinion, we should all live in a world where we are still acknowledged for our achievements, even if they are small. When we are acknowledged, this creates a chemical reaction inside us, which releases endorphins, and makes us happy and proud of ourselves. However, as we live in a busy world, with so many distractions going on and other people being too busy living their own lives, it is important, and sometimes necessary, that we do this ourselves. At times, it is up to you to reward yourself, and to give yourself the praise that you deserve, this will keep you on the right track and keep your mind healthy. It is important also to reward yourself in times of failure, because *failure is good*, it demonstrates to yourself that you have made the effort, you can learn from the mistakes made, and *try again*.

There are far too many people who will love to hear when things do not go right for you, believe me or believe me not but this is true. The reasons for this are firstly due to jealousy, at your ambition and your desire to change your life. Secondly, it is their doubt in you as to your capability to make these changes happen. They may say to you "You won't be able to do that". In most cases, we will then believe them, and start repeating back all the negative disempowering words that we hear, "can't, won't, don't". We fear that others may think we are becoming inferior to them and will not want us to look better than them. But nobody is better than anyone, and everyone is equal. Some people do not have the knowhow to create a better life for themselves. In my opinion, and from my own experience, it starts with how we talk to ourselves, who we surround ourselves with, and how we are rewarding ourselves at each achievement milestone that we reach. The more you continue rewarding yourself, the more you will feel good about *the person that you are becoming*. Treat yourself with the respect, love, and dignity that you deserve. Self-praise and self-rewarding are not crimes, they are just a sign of your love for yourself, and all you have, and will achieve.

Change and Letting Go
by Maria Farkasova

For me, it was always important how people perceived me and what they thought of me. As such, my life was very reactive. My decisions were not based on what I thought was right, I made them according to other people's expectations. I didn't like myself. I thought for a long time that I was not good enough. I constantly compared myself to others. I didn't trust myself. I remember a very passive period in my life. I didn't know which direction to go in. When I asked other people's opinion, I got answers, but I still couldn't make decisions. I was afraid to make a mistake, make an incorrect decision. I wasn't playing the main character in my life, only extras. I didn't feel alive. I became a victim, even though I wasn't born one.

I felt a desire for change several times in my life. It was a repeated pattern. 'What change do I want?' was a question I regularly asked myself. Looking back now, I wasn't always aware that outside change starts inside. I was a dreamer, always with my head in the clouds. I was one of those people who wanted to change the world. Then one day I realised that I needed to change my own world first and one day, maybe, I would return to my desire to make the world a better place for other people.

I decided that if I was to create change, I needed to move far away from my family. I loved my family, but I didn't want my life to be like theirs. I wanted something more. Of course, I didn't realise at the time that even though I was travelling alone, I would take a big part of them with me. I didn't realise that a change of external environment doesn't necessarily bring the change you expect. It can be an adventure at the beginning, seeing new things, getting to know new people and experiencing a new culture, but after a while when you settle down, a desire for something new awakens again, because the last one didn't bring the desired outcome. There are many different types of change – you can change a partner, work, accommodation, your hairstyle, etc. The question is, how long will you be satisfied?

Coaching helped me in my search for a change. I volunteered to be a guinea pig for a friend's friend. No, my life didn't change radically straight away but change came gradually. I changed my focus and let go of the past. It was what I needed. It was a beginning and an opening for change. Instead of living in my past, I started to concentrate on my future. I couldn't change the past, but the future was in front of me to create, a blank book of life with different unlimited possibilities.

A simple coaching exercise really helped me, called the Wheel of Life. It represents life like a circle, divided into different categories that represent areas of life, such as money, career and relationships. You score yourself (0-10) on how satisfied you are in those areas. At that time, I was very focused on spirituality, however by doing this exercise I realised that, for me to be happy, maybe I needed to be more balanced and invest into other areas as well, areas that I had previously ignored. To progress, that wheel needed to turn smoothly and that could only happen with balance. I learned that by identifying and improving one or two areas of life, it impacts other areas. I asked myself 'What change would make a difference? What one thing can I change that would have the biggest impact?' I started to feel that my life could change and there was a way out of the 'trap'. I realised I had options.

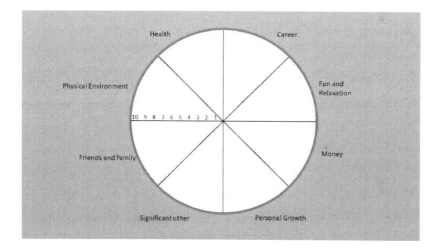

In fairy tales, fairies present a child with gifts that predict their destiny. For them to fulfil that destiny, they usually have to fight for it. In real life, we are highly influenced by our family, our circumstances and the environment we are born into, so our destiny feels almost predetermined by those influencers. That said, it's a common expectation that we will lead a similar life to our family. Have you ever felt stuck in your family conditions and expectations? I had that feeling, and maybe because of that, I wanted to spread my wings and fly.

In my country we have a New Year's Day tradition, that says we shouldn't eat meat from a bird with feathers. One says happiness will fly out, others say that a family member will leave the nest. I wanted to experience adventures. I felt too protected at home. I wanted to have space to learn and make mistakes. I couldn't wait until tomorrow. I couldn't wait to be eighteen. I just wanted to open my wings and fly. I was still dependent on my mother, but I wanted to fly.

Over thirteen years ago I moved to Ireland and it really became obvious that I was carrying my family with me wherever I was going. I had a dream about a child born with tattoos all over its body. I believe that values and beliefs are like invisible tattoos. They are not on us, but they are rooted deeply in us. I don't believe we are born with them, but we consciously or subconsciously absorb them and once there, it is difficult to erase them or change them.

I was born in Central Europe, in a Socialist country into a Catholic family. Even when I was growing in a loving family, with my mum and grandparents, love had its conditions. My parents broke up when I was a child. As a result, I felt it was safer to stay single than settle like my Mum. "We are poor, and we will stay poor. Hard work, loyalty, service to others, everyone is more important than me." They were or still are some of the marks in my mind. Some of them were more challenging to live with than others.

My father not being present in my life influenced me more than I realised. At about ten years old, I blocked my emotions and I wouldn't allow myself to cry. It took a long time to let that go until I decided to unblock my emotions and feel the pain of his absence. Now I know, blocking my emotions was a way of protection. In that situation, I did the best that I could.

Maybe you experienced something similar in your life, a time where you felt miserable or felt like a victim, a victim of life circumstances, family or your upbringing. Maybe you felt sorry for yourself. Is there a way out of this? I used to think, what if I would be born into a different family? What if I moved abroad? What if I left my job? I blamed myself and others for my mistakes. I reacted to others' decisions and wondered where it would lead me. I expected that life would make the decision for me. In the process, my life was passing me by.

I lived inside a bubble, a bubble created partially by my family and partially by me. Nothing could get in from the outside and nothing could harm me, but my world wasn't colourful. Nothing was growing inside. Some people saw me as a boring person with no sense of fun, that I wasn't alive. I had created a protective wall to avoid emotion, and life was miserable as a result.

I concluded that for me to be happy, I needed to feel again, and I allowed myself to go there. You can imagine what happened. Yes, I experienced a lot pain. However, with support I was able to process it. When I look back now, there was a lot more joy than I thought. I just had to feel it all to understand that.

If you think of a caterpillar, it needs to go into its own cocoon to transform into a butterfly. I believe that emotion is like that, it helps us to grow, if we accept it with trust and believe that there is a light at the end of the tunnel. If we don't accept it, and instead hold onto the negatives, the blame and the anger without forgiving and letting go, we can become bitter.

I always had a problem with forgiveness, and it kept me stuck, but when we don't forgive, we resent and feel sorry for ourselves, which is a wasted life. In my experience, you become a victim when you hold onto negative emotions and when you feed them. I learned to be more curious about negative emotions. If you feel fear, anger, sadness or guilt, ask yourself what positive intentions has this negative emotion. Then try to find some other, more positive way to fulfil that. When you feel a negative emotion, try to find out in yourself, why you reacted this way, learn from it and let it go.

I believe our external world reflects our internal one. In the last few years I learned a lot about mind over matter. At one of my Neuro Linguistic Programming (NLP) coaching courses, a course that studies the mind-body link, I broke a 1 cm thick wooden board. You might have seen it in martial arts. You must concentrate, hit the board in the right way and it breaks, however not always at the first attempt. Preparation might take a month. At the course, we had less than one hour to do it. We had to get into right state of breathing deeply, focusing, believing and then breaking the board. I didn't find it as simple as some. I found it almost impossible. I usually overanalyse and overthink everything and so it was the same this time too. T. Harv Eker says, *"As you do anything, you do everything."* It took me a while until I found the right posture and I decided to go for it. I hit my fingers the first time. I concentrated on the board extensively while wondering if it is possible, but I saw others do it. On the second attempt, the board broke, not because of my strength.

When I touched the board, my eyes were closed, and I kept repeating to myself. "There is no board. There is no obstacle."

In the past I wished for challenges. Now I create positive challenges for myself. I deal with different challenges every day. If I feel it's too much, I often think about the board exercise and keep telling myself, "There is no obstacle". Maybe some people would see some of my challenges as problems, but it is easier to deal with them under this label.

We are aware of experiences that are happening around us and that we are part of. Our lives are very self-centred. There was a time in my life, when I was walking with my head down and was concentrating only on me. I felt bad and I couldn't see a way out. One day, I lifted my head and saw all the beauty around me. I got out from my vicious circle. I realised that there are many things I need to be grateful for. For my family, for example. I am who I am because of their support, and my friends are here for me, if I need them. I changed my perception.

I always felt, I needed to fight for my identity and place in the world. For my whole life I felt I needed to be strong. Listening to the song, *Baby Don't Cry*, and looking at a poster of Muhammad Ali on my wall – I tried to hold my life firmly in my hands and everything that it might bring. It felt like I had built a house from playing cards that could fall with the slightest move. I couldn't hold it. I had to let it fall and build it again, on a new base, from a new material, and make it more stable. I now know that it's okay to let go and not be in control. I can take off my boxing gloves.

I had to stop blaming my family for my failures and take responsibility for my life. I prayed the Serenity prayer:

'Grant me the serenity to accept the things I cannot change, the courage to change the things I can, and the wisdom to know the difference.'

Forgiveness was an important stepping stone in my search for meaningful change. I was brought up in a religious way – How often should I forgive someone…? Seven times? No, not seven times, but seventy-seven times! I always knew it was important to forgive, but there was a period when I could not do it and a time when I didn't know how to forgive. Now I have a different view on forgiveness. I understand that forgiveness is a decision. I probably forgave "seventy-seven times", but only at a head level. I didn't let go the negative emotions such as sadness, hurt or anger. I couldn't move forward. I must admit that forgiveness was a selfish act for me. I wanted a change and I knew, I had to start from the inside. I didn't write letters to people who hurt me. My realisation helped me, that in every situation we act the best as we can. Try to put yourself in the shoes of the other person who hurt you. What would you see? What would you hear? What would you feel? They look at the world through their experiences, beliefs and values. We are all vulnerable. It's human to make mistakes, and it's common that people who are closest to us, hurt us most. In fact, I found it most difficult to forgive myself. I now understand that forgiveness is a decision and a process. Let me tell you a story.

There was a woman who took a walk up a hill with a full backpack. She got to a place where she couldn't do it anymore. She was walking much slower than usual. She had to sit down and take a rest. After a while she opened her backpack and looked inside it. It was full of stones. Always when something bad happened, she picked one and put it into her backpack. She started to look at the stones – one was from a time when she had an argument with her friend, the next one was from a time when she wasn't successful at a job interview, a big one reminded her of her parents' break up. She closed the backpack, stood up, and took a few steps. Feeling the weight of her load, she had to stop again. She thought, 'What if I take out one stone and leave it on side the road? And the next one? What about this big one? I definitely won't forget it.' Suddenly it was easier to walk. She continued leaving more stones on the side of the road. She started to see the world around her. She felt free and started to run up the hill. She hasn't felt so good for a long time. Her name was Maria.

We all have those stones that we carry. I used to think I wasn't good enough, I thought I was too old when I was about thirty years old, that I was too fat when I was a size 12, that my English wasn't good enough etc. I found a notebook from a self-development course on which I had described myself. Now I ask myself 'How could I see myself that way? Why was my self-esteem so low?' I am older now, I put on few dress sizes and my self-image is healthier.

Forgiveness is an essential step towards healing and freedom. If you are to create long lasting change, you must let go and forgive whatever or whoever hurt you. Carrying those stones will weigh you down!

One of my negative beliefs was that I was not good enough. I just couldn't let it go and placed blame on others for that belief. As part of my self-development, I decided to take a leaf out of Louise Hayes' book and began affirming positive phrases to myself. Admittedly at the beginning, it was a challenge as I didn't believe good things about myself, but it refocused my thoughts. I also created a vision board (pictures of the life I wanted) and wrote on it "I am good enough". When I was thinking that I am not good enough, too old, too fat or that my English is not good enough, I told and visualised myself that "I am enough". I kept repeating it over and over. Now I see that I was comparing myself to others my whole life. I tried to fit in, be like others, but we are all different and unique. After a while I stopped seeing myself through the critical eyes of other people. I started to see myself though the eyes of God. If you don't believe in God, try to see yourself through the eyes of people who like you, support you, and believe in you. It makes a big difference.

Having done a lot of work on myself, now I can look at myself in the mirror and smile at myself. I learned to love myself. I like my eyes, even though they are short-sighted, they enable me to see world and people around me. Depending on the colour of my clothes, they are sometimes grey and sometimes have a blue shade. Even though I have some extra kilograms, my body functions well. My feet take me where I want. My hands can do different activities. My brain can process information. How people see me has stopped being so important to me. I have grown from being a small shy unconfident Maria to becoming a person I want to be. Become a person who knows your self-worth and accept yourself. I decided to rewrite my story, walk with courage, be grateful for what I have. I decided to wake up! I ask you to do the same for your own sake.

We all received different gifts and God painted us in different colours. I would like to bring my gift of uniqueness to the world. I would like to be myself, even if I am still not sure what it means specifically. However, I remind myself that life is a gift from God and not trusting myself, exploring my gifts and abilities, is like putting it into the corner and not opening it. Now I am opening my gift and learning to know myself.

"Our deepest fear is not that we are inadequate. Our deepest fear is that we are powerful beyond measure. It is our light, not our darkness that most frightens us. We ask ourselves, who am I to be brilliant, gorgeous, talented, fabulous? Actually, who are you not to be? You are a child of God. Your playing small does not serve the world. There is nothing enlightened about shrinking so that other people won't feel insecure around you. We are all meant to shine, as children do. We were born to make manifest the glory of God that is within us. It's not just in some of us, it's in everyone. And as we let our own light to shine, we unconsciously give other people permission to do the same. As we are liberated from our own fear, our presence automatically liberates others."

- Marianne Williamson

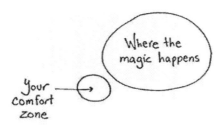

You might have seen this picture before. For me it represents that "magic" form of a change. I am curious what is outside. For me that place outside of the comfort zone is a symbol of taking risk, embracing the unknown, excitement, living without limits, adventure, freedom, fulfilment, confidence, challenge connected to growth and change. When we find courage to do things outside our comfort zone, our comfort zone grows, and we grow with it. On the other side, in our youth, we often want to change the world. When we get in contact with reality, we realise that it's not so simple. The comfort zone can get smaller.

Most of my life I was afraid to fail, so I only very occasionally tried new things. Quite often, my family did things for me. They did it faster and better. As I was growing up, I was afraid to make mistakes. In order to grow, I had to stop being afraid to fail and start being afraid not to try. This was a huge shift for me. I had to stop making excuses and start to live with no regrets. Sometimes I am more successful than other times. There are still areas of my life where I don't have courage to change anything yet. I am learning to take small baby steps. I am not sure where I am going all the time, but I am actively moving forward.

When I finished University, I hadn't set any goals. I didn't have a concrete plan in place for what I wanted to do with my life. I started to set up challenges for myself, stepping stones that could push me forward. One of the first ones was running. I printed a plan – a couch to 5 km and bought a few books about running but I didn't get too far. So, I got a coach. I started walking and continued with interval running and finally I was able to run 5 km, slowly, but as my coach said, when I have two feet in the air at the same time, I am running. I confess, I didn't trust myself at the beginning. I was never able to run more than few metres, but I learned to trust myself and move step by step towards my goal. I have never heard so many encouraging words from anyone, but it worked. I needed external approval. In a short period of time I was able to run 5km. My running wasn't much faster than my walking, but it was a success for me. The first race I signed up for wasn't 5km but a 13km charity run in the Wicklow Mountains. I didn't know what to expect. After a short flat terrain there was a steep hill. I walked towards the end of the group. Surprisingly most of the track was uphill. It required more effort than I expected but I didn't give up. I concentrated on the goal and finished the race and I didn't come last.

The following year I signed up for 5km and 10km runs and when I managed those, I signed up for a half marathon. I knew approximately how long it would take me to run 10km and even if I would walk the rest, I had to finish within the time limit. I wanted to test my limits and slowly I started to trust myself more. At the beginning I never expected to participate in a half marathon race. I took a picture of myself standing on the podium for winners. I felt like a winner. I stretched my goal. I was imagining myself crossing the finish line.

When one of the presenters at a self-development course I attended, talked about the *Tough Mudder* obstacle race I added it into my bucket list. When I saw it being promoted in my gym, I signed up before checking what I was letting myself in for. I attended the preparation training only once. I returned to my old way of thinking, of comparing myself to others. I thought others were much fitter than me and were much better at exercise, I couldn't imagine myself completing the race. I felt really scared but I didn't let it stop me. I did it anyway. I couldn't, I didn't, let fear control me. It was a victory for me to participate. I was the only one from my gym, who did the half-track option. I must admit, I skipped some of the obstacles, but I didn't have to prove myself anymore. At *Tough Mudder* there were some water obstacles and after years I decided to learn to swim again. Until now, I had a great respect for water but an equally great fear, but

I don't feel that overwhelming fear any more. I still have to keep working on this, but I have taken the first step and after that have continued to take many more. Now I need to practice and keep conquering my fears. It's like in Guillaume Apollinaire's poem:

"Come to the edge. We can't. We're afraid. Come to the edge. We can't. We will fall. Come to the edge. And they came. And he pushed them. And they flew."

I don't consider myself an expert on goal setting but I am learning what works for me. It seems, like setting bigger goals and dividing them into small pieces works for me. Taking part in different activities that I thought I could never do makes me feel more involved in life. Now I believe that there is no such thing as failure, only feedback or a learning experience. Is there something you would like to do in your life? Do you have something on your mind for a while? I learned that if I think about something for a long time, I just need to decide, do I want to do it or not and if not, I need to stop thinking about it.

I laugh when my colleague told me, "I have a New Year's resolution for you. Don't sign up for the impossible." My response was, to quote Henry Ford, *"Whether you think you can, or you think you can't, you're right."*

I believe if somebody else did it, I can do it too. It's about perception. Some of my goals might be easily achievable for somebody else but a stretch for me. I am not ready for some challenges yet. However, I believe we are either growing or dying, therefore I have a new project in mind, challenging for me now.

I admit, I am not the type of person who lets other people into my private space. I am not that type who would have shared feelings. Even now, although not as much as before, to get to know me requires interest and patience. I usually don't share my weaknesses and struggles. To write about myself feels like being naked in front of people. It feels very uncomfortable. Writing was on my bucket list. If I didn't say yes to this opportunity, I don't think I would ever have started writing. I was focusing for a long time on the undesired outcome, the consequences of possible failure and this caused my motivation to move my energy *away from* my goal. To complete this challenge, I had to turn my focus *towards* the possible benefits and stay curious to where this will bring me.

When I learned more about self-compassion and specifically connection to the heart, I realised this was the missing piece for me. I spoke to myself in a critical voice a lot. I wouldn't tell a friend, what I was telling myself. Sometimes that critical voice wasn't mine, it belonged to somebody from my friends or family. I was brought up to have self-compassion for others but not towards myself. Can I give, what I don't have? If I don't love and accept myself, how can I expect it from others? Now, when I notice that I am thinking something negative about myself, or in general, I think a positive thought instead, or at least I try. Inspired by *m*BIT coaching (a process of aligning and harnessing the power of your multiple intelligences, head, heart and gut "brains", through a series of practical coaching methods and exercises), I kept practicing breathing on a daily basis. There are different techniques but this one is about balanced breathing. It is continuous breathing without any breaks, where inbreath and outbreath are the same length. Breathe in on the count of six and then breathe out on the count of six. When I do this for at least two and a half minutes a day, I find myself being more balanced and better able to deal with all the challenges that life brings. I remember staying calm when my little cousin's son spilled tea on the carpet. Was this a result of breathing? I believe it was. I think a lot and overthink everything. In addition to paying attention to my thoughts, I have started to be aware of my heart and gut. In relation to a specific issue, I ask my heart, 'What do I truly feel and desire? What do I value and find important?' I find it helpful to put my hand on my heart. It was trying to get my attention many times. "Hello, I am here. I want to be listened to." I heard a silent voice from my heart, I just ignored it. Not anymore! I also ask my gut 'What do I hunger for or identify with?' I am learning to accept my mistakes, to make them is to be human. I finally realised that I don't need to be perfect. Nobody is.

In my transformation from being a victim to a victor, I realised that life is a journey and I am learning to enjoy it every day. As a child I couldn't wait for tomorrow. Now I enjoy the present and I am curious what tomorrow will bring. If I would compare life to a run, it would be a long-distance run, not a sprint. It's about moving forward. For me, life is about becoming the best version of ourselves. Even if my life is not progressing according to my expectations, I have decided to be happy and do things that make me feel happy and alive. I got many slaps from life, I fell many times on my bottom, but I always got up and kept going. Some people might not be aware of my transformation, because externally my life might not appear to have changed dramatically, however I feel good. Maybe it changed more than I think. I have great friends, I am experiencing new things, I have a job that I enjoy and supportive colleagues. Every day I concentrate on what I am grateful for. I changed my perception about my origins. Because of my family's influence I became who I am. That resilience and strength not to give up comes from them. Even when I am searching for my own way in life, my mum is still the most important person for me. My whole life is an adventure now. I don't need to plan all my steps and have everything under control. I like the surprises. I am rewriting my story. I am leaving my negative believes behind me and instead telling myself that I am good enough. I am enough. I am worth it. I am happy. I am fulfilled. I don't need external approval anymore, I found it inside, as well as the answers to my questions. I find time every day for a few minutes silence, prayer, breathing and reading. If I don't have time for all of them, I do at least one. I feel better starting my day in more proactive way.

From Tony Robbins', *Unleash the Power Within*, I learned that our internal state and body posture are very closely connected. When I felt like a victim, I was carrying my head down, it didn't feel good. Now, I keep my head high. It's important for me to keep my energy levels high. I find going to a gym class or a prayer meeting helpful. Music brought a different dimension into my life. I tried singing, viola, ukulele and Gamelan (traditional Indonesian music) recently. It didn't matter how bad I felt, my dynamic changed, and I suddenly started to feel better. The Gamelan class was like meditation or mindfulness for two hours per week. I had to switch off and concentrate solely on the music. I am aware of the importance of being in a positive state. When I lose it, I can return into it simply by changing my posture, laughing or 'shaking the ass' as I learned at the course. Things happen, and my life is richer. I proved to myself that limiting beliefs can change. Our destiny is not predetermined, we are co-creators of our lives. There are multiple ways to find fulfilment and purpose in life.

What is going to be your first step on your journey towards a happier and more fulfilled life, knowing yourself and showing your colours?

Claiming back Your Power
by Jennifer Byrne

Too many "Ifs", too many "Whens", too many "Sorrys", too many "Never Agains", too many "Promises", too many "Lies" and "One more times", all before I knew that actions speak louder than promises ever do.

Frothing at the mouth, that bent finger pointing at me, I feel a spray of his saliva splash onto my face. The strong scent of his Versace cologne mixed in with the smells of brandy and cigarettes lingering in the air. Eyes wild, the monster within raising that ugly, evil head yet again. In a fit of rage the venom continues to roll off his tongue, wicked, evil, vicious words, the demon really is out tonight. I can feel my heart pounding hard, I wonder can he hear it or even see it through my chest? Staring at the clock on the wall, watching the second hand just ticking away. How long more do I have to listen to this, it's late and I need to be up early to get the kids ready for school. I really wish he would just hit me, get it over and done with, but I know in my heart and soul this can go on for another couple of hours at least. He is only warming up, he's like a broken record at this stage, hurling the abusive threats against me, my family, my friends, we are all stupid "Irish fools". We all come from nothing, we are nobodies, that have nothing, broke ass fools who would be nothing without him. I've been dying to go to the toilet for over forty minutes now, I don't think I can hold it much longer, so I really need to ask him can I go to the bathroom. Taking a deep breath in, I blurt out the words 'Please, can I go use the toilet?' Grabbing me by the wrist he drags me to the bathroom. I have to leave the door open, he's standing there over me, watching me, that ugly, stupid grin on his face, glass of brandy in his hand and blowing the cigarette smoke in my direction. I hate cigarette smoke, I don't smoke. Looking at the plastic fish lined up along the bathtub fills my heart with a little glow, that warm fuzzy feeling of love, the fond memories of only a few hours beforehand, my little men smiling up at me as they splashed around in the bath before bedtime.

Suddenly brought back to the realization of the nightmare I'm experiencing right now, yet another stream of disgusting abuse hurled at me, nasty, vulgar words aimed at my vaginal area. The constant battle with myself to either stay quiet, endure the toxicity of his verbal abuse which can go on and on, meaning I probably won't get any sleep or answer back which will more than likely result in his fist in my face but at least I might get some sleep. I didn't get the chance to make the decision this time as I feel the hard wallop to the side of my head. The stars appear first, feeling dizzy from the impact, the ringing in my ears, my mouth is so dry. That gut-wrenching feeling of nausea in the pit of my tummy, the sting of the slap getting more intense. Telling myself 'Don't cry Jennifer, don't give him the satisfaction of seeing you cry again.' Another wallop to the back of my head, the weakness runs through my body and I fall to the floor. Curled up in a ball I can feel the coldness of the floor against my body. Trembling with fear inside, yet I lay there motionless, afraid to move or even breath. I hope this is over now, I really need to sleep. I don't know how long I've been here for, I'm shivering with the cold and I'm so thirsty. Then the tears fall, I can't stop, I'm in so much pain, emotionally, physically, my heart, my spirit broken. I no longer know who this person is. The waves of anger, fear, disgust, shame, guilt, despair, loneliness, resentment, all at once, I can't deal with this.

Startled by the knock at the door, I can hear voices, he barges in and tells me the guards are at the door. One of the neighbours must have called them again. I can see how they look at me, that look of pity in their eyes, shaking their heads, knowing only too well that I won't press charges. They leave, I can hear the birds singing, yet another sleepless night. Looking in the mirror at this pale reflection, eyes red and puffy from crying, I no longer know the person staring back at me. Who is this girl? Where has Jennifer gone? Then the ritual begins trying to disguise the bruising on my face, using eyeshadow under the foundation will work wonders, trust me I've had plenty of practice. As if covering them up will make all the pain go away, like who am I fooling only myself. He says he loves me, so why do I feel so unloved? The sound of his snoring, sleeping deeply without a care in the world, fills me with rage. How can he sleep after what he has done? I tiptoe passed the sitting room where he is sleeping, the smell of the stale cigarette smoke wafting in the air. I go through the motions of yet another day walking on eggshells, living on edge. I hope he wakes up in a better mood today.

After twelve years of that life I finally broke free. It's April 2011, my younger brother hands me the keys to the new lock he has installed to my front door before he heads off on his travels to Australia and right then in that very moment, I knew life could only get better. So, I hear you ask the question, how did I finally break free? The answer to that, with great difficulty. But I did. I am now a confident, happy, empowered woman. I will take you through my journey but for now let me start at the beginning.

I'm the eldest of five children, raised in a working-class family. My dad, a hardworking man, always had total adoration, respect and love for my mother and still does to this day. He would come home from work and hand his wage packet to my mother and never took a penny for himself. I remember when he even worked an extra job on a Saturday with the coal man so that he could take my mother out to the local pub on a Saturday night. I didn't grow up in a violent household, there were never any raised, heated arguments between my parents, and the only way we would have known as kids if they had fallen out, would be if my mother gave my father the silent treatment for a day or two. So, how the hell did I end up at hands of an abusive man for twelve years of my life?

Let me ask you a question, have you ever found yourself in a relationship that you know is never really going to work out after you become parents for the first time? All you mothers out there get me, right? Your outlook on life changes when you become a mother for the first time and that little bundle of joy becomes your priority. When I first met my eldest son's Dad we clicked and got on like a house on fire. Both young, carefree and the only thing that mattered was getting dressed up to go out at the weekend after working all week. He was my first long term relationship and like any young couple in what I thought was love at the time, we decided to move in together and rented our first apartment. After three years together, I discovered I was pregnant. I was shocked at first but that soon turned into excitement. After our son was born, we both did our best as parents and his dad idolised him. I was twenty-four years old and his dad a year younger than me, so both still very young. Cracks began to show in the relationship. Weekends stuck at home while his dad seemed to continue his socialising like he did before becoming a dad. He started missing days off work, losing jobs, lying about money, not paying rent, etc. This pressure on top of being young parents put a lot of strain on the relationship. When my son was two years old, I had enough of the arguments over money and his dad's drinking habits, so I decided that his dad and I were better off apart. I was working full time as a Production Supervisor for a Healthcare company, so I knew I could financially adjust to single parenthood and his dad's family were always very supportive and helped a lot, taking my son at weekends and summer holidays.

Fast forward to 1999, I'm twenty-six years old and I have a two-year-old son. A tall, dark, handsome man began working on the production line that I was supervising. He was charming. I was enjoying the attention he gave me and the flirtatious banter. After been in a relationship where drink and football seemed to be more important than me, this attention and charm attracted me to him. Totally different to my previous partner, not into football or drinking with the lads in the pub, or so I thought, only later to discover he was more into women and staying out drinking all night at parties! Wined and dined in fancy restaurants, making me feel special, he even escorted me to the ladies on a night out to make sure I was okay and that no drunken fools were annoying me (his words), thinking to myself, how cute is that! I should have seen the warning signs, but I was blinded by his charm. You see, they do that first, I suppose, to brainwash you in a way, but little did I know that this was just the start of my life been controlled totally by another person. He questioned what I wore, where I shopped, who I spoke to, he told me how to act, even down to what I ate and drank at times. Everything controlled. If only I had known what lay ahead for the next twelve years. But there is no point living with what ifs. I believe that everything in life happens for a reason and moulds us into the person we are today. I was meant to meet him, otherwise I would never have had my second beautiful baby boy. A whirlwind romance, pregnant after only five months together, and already he had me where he wanted me. I was a single mother, easy prey, I didn't have the freedom of a single girl, and now I was pregnant with a child for him. I was trapped and vulnerable. I should have known never to trust a man that carried more than one phone. Thinking back, I was so naïve and really hadn't a clue. The verbal abuse had already begun, he would come and go as he pleased, expecting me to be at his beckon call. I was pregnant with his child, so I was his now. The first physical assault happened when I was carrying his child. I was seven months pregnant and we were on a night out, as always with his people. His friend was just chatting to me (at least one of them was being friendly) and speaking English to me. Being surrounded by full blown conversations for hours in a language I didn't speak used to really irritate me. I used to sit there feeling like a fool, you know that feeling when you're in a room full of people, yet you feel so alone. On the way home, I got accused of flirting with his friend and he kicked me from behind. Then the apologies, 'I'm so sorry it will never happen again.' He went out and bought me some new clothes the following day, the vicious cycle of abuse had begun.

Lying in bed three weeks before I'm due to give birth, on my own yet again, I really hope he starts to stay over when it's nearer my due date. My phone rings, I don't recognise the number, but I answer it, maybe he has changed his phone again. All I can hear is a lady screaming down the phone calling me all the names under the sun. I'm confused, I don't know this lady, how does she know me? She then tells me that she had a baby girl a week ago and yes, you guessed it, he was the father! He denied it, of course, she was just a crazy ex-girlfriend who was jealous of me because he chose to be with me and not her! I should be grateful right? After all he chose me over another girl. The target of his manipulation, I accept what is, even if I totally understand what's happening, but I can't say no because of threats.

Do you ever feel like you are living your life with blinkers on, you know that feeling where you're just existing but not actually living? On the outside you're smiling but on the inside you're crumbling. You go through the motions of everyday life, accepting situations whatever they might be, at home, in the workplace, relationships, only to come to the realisation that you have adapted to these environments, you have become trapped, conditioned and then BOOM, you're in way too deep. I know your probably saying to yourself why didn't she just leave that first time he kicked her? The truth is nobody really knows how they will react or respond to any situation or traumatic event in life until you witness it first-hand. Abuse causes our personality to change. Our personalities refer to both who we are at our core, our true core values, and how others perceive us to be. Nothing challenges our personalities or our core values more than living a lie. It confuses our thoughts and emotions. We see ourselves behave in ways we never thought we'd behave. The resulting emotions of anxiety, fear and emotional pain reflect our sense of losing ourselves and disappearing because our actions and words are no longer true to our core values or who we really are. You get to a stage where all emotions are suppressed. You know that feeling, you smile but your eyes, the windows to your soul, tell a different story. You are no longer you.

After my son was born, things got a lot worse. Now we still weren't living together, he only moved in with me when he no longer could afford his apartment. I never actually asked him to move in, he just took the liberty of arriving at my door one day with all his belongings. This was around two years after my son was born. It was difficult trying to juggle two small children and working fulltime too, especially when you don't have the support of a loving partner. I decided to job share for a while working a three-day week, but after nine months of job sharing, the company I was working for began to cut the workforce and, unfortunately because I was only part time, I was let go. This was when I really began to feel isolated. I no longer had the connection with work colleagues, I was at home with two young children. I had no income, only a social welfare payment. He loved that because I relied on him helping me out. He would come and go as he pleased, stay for a day or two, and then go back to his apartment. Now don't get me wrong, there were some good times over the years too and I suppose looking back, that cycle of abuse was probably another reason why I stayed so long too. It's like they're playing mind games with you. He could be so nice for weeks, even months, buying food, helping with bills, buying things for the children. Things would be going so well because I was just at home, no contact with anyone apart from him and his friends, but a whole different story if I wanted to go out anywhere or meet up with friends or family. He would always make it so difficult, it got to a stage where I just didn't bother because of the stress it caused. If he had his way, he would have had me at home, tied to the kitchen sink with another two or three children.

I remember the day I received the letter from the council telling me that I would be allocated a house back in my hometown. I was thrilled as I would be closer to my family and friends. My eldest son was in school and my youngest was in preschool. I had the mornings free and I decided to start doing the fitness classes in the local community centre. This was the start of me gaining back some control and doing something for me. Little did I know how much of an impact this would have on my future! I lived for the three classes a week, I loved the coffee and the chats with the other women afterwards and for those few hours I felt like me again. After a year or so a part time position for a Creche supervisor was advertised at the centre and I decided to apply for it. This didn't go down so well, the usual, "Who is going to mind my son? You're not leaving my son with just any fool." But at this stage I had it all worked out. If I got the job, both my sons would be in primary school, so I didn't need to look for childcare. I got the job and remained there for two years. It worked out perfectly and when the children where on midterm breaks or holidays I would book them into the sports camps that the community centre ran. Of course, there where stressful times and I remember having to bring them with me to work on the odd occasion because he wouldn't be around to look after them and

I wasn't allowed to leave his son with just anyone without his say so.

Life got a little easier as the kids got a little older and there were good times but of course so many bad times too. After the creche job I decided to go back to education and I signed up with the local VTOS centre for a business course along with French and Spanish. I was doing well, I was enjoying the social element of the course and keeping up with my new love of weight training. Both where added bonuses in my life (apart from my kids) as they were something to focus on for me for those few hours a day and take my mind off what was happening at home. To the outside world it might have looked like I was a confident, happy person, but like the bruises, I had plenty of practice at pretending everything was fine. I was so unhappy. He was travelling back and forth to Africa and would stay there for four to six weeks at least once or twice a year. I loved it when he was gone. The house was so peaceful, and I was happy out with the kids. When you're in that constant cycle of abuse you get so used to ignoring how you really feel, always just pretending. One year we all went to Africa for his friend's wedding. That was a good year and we were getting on so well, I was thirty-four, I felt happy in myself for once and was even getting a little broody, considering having another child! The universe was on my side then, because something just in the back of my mind soon brought an end to that idea. As always, those good times were always brought to an abrupt end. After we got back another brutal attack happened, this time I ended up with a cracked rib from the force of the push against the kitchen table.

Physically I was always there as a mother for my boys, cooking, cleaning, the usual grind of daily life, but I was in a state of emotional turmoil. I was just a shell of my former self, numb, battling with my own self-loathing daily. How could I possibly be emotionally stable for my children when I was an emotional wreck? I blamed myself for a very long time for the difficult times I had with my eldest son in his teenage years (that's a story for another day), but in hindsight I know that I was doing the best I could in extremely difficult circumstances. I had to let go of all that regret. My sons know how much love I have for them, I might not have always shown it but in the end, it was that love I had for them that gave me the strength and courage to finally break free.

It's mid-2009, I'm sitting down on the sofa, just about to tuck into my dinner, it's a nice steak dinner too, with the creamy mash, fried mushrooms, onions and peppercorn sauce. I've been looking forward to it all day. The kids are settled down for the evening, up in their rooms, more than likely playing on the PlayStation. It seems like a typical evening in any home, right? He's upstairs in bed on his phone, he's been up there now for most of the day, I can't really tell you what the conversation is about (I never really could understand his language), I just picked up on a few words and phrases over the years. I can tell from the tone of his voice he's arguing, sure what's new? Not a day goes by when he's not arguing with someone on the phone. I'm sick of the sound of his voice, he has a very loud voice, so I can never escape it. I've had a few mouthfuls of my food, I can hear him come down the stairs. I hope he's going out somewhere, at least then I can relax for a few hours. My heart sinks when I see the door swing open, the ranting begins, he's angry because I'm sitting down eating and didn't offer him his food. The last mouthful that I just had stuck in my throat, then the loud smash as my dinner is flung against the wall. I'm stuck to the sofa, watching my lovely dinner slide down the wall in front of me. In my head I'm screaming "Fuck you, you fucking prick", but I just sit there in silence, heart racing, hands sweaty yet cold to touch, that feeling in the pit of your tummy when you're really frightened. He's hovering over me and then, wallop! I feel that sharp whack to the side of my head. The stars appear again, I'm feeling dizzy, but I can just about make out the vision of my eldest son standing at the door. He has a kitchen knife in his hand and he's shouting at him 'Leave my mam alone!' That was it, I knew there and then this had to stop. He was only twelve years old, a child, my precious child. I'm his mother, I should be protecting him, keeping him from harm and from all the bad people in this world. No child should ever have to witness this. I knew something had to change.

I can't remember exactly how long I left the splatters of that dinner on the wall, but I know they remained there for a long while before I cleaned them off. They were a constant reminder along with the haunting vision of my son that made me stick by the decision, that something had to change. I made a promise to myself that I had to break free. I knew it wasn't going to be easy, but I was determined that I wasn't going to talk myself out of it this time round. And yes, of course, I'm sure as hell you can only imagine, the consequences of breaking free scared the living daylights out of me but I knew I had to do it. So many thoughts running round my head, the only way I can describe it is, that they felt like a washing machine on a spin cycle, constantly spinning around and around. 'What if this happens? What will people think? How will I ever get beyond the shame? A single mother again, two sons, two different fathers, one white child, one mixed race child, slut, people will judge me, typical single mother living in a council estate, living off a social welfare payment, stupid, sure no one will ever want me, dumbass bitch, she must of enjoyed all the drama, if she stayed with him for so long, that's what she gets for getting involved with an African man, she must of known, sure they're known for beating women, idiot, fool, good for nothing.' All those thoughts constantly trying to stop me, talk myself out of it, you see, I was seeing myself through his eyes now, years of all that verbal abuse had me believing that I was all those thoughts. I knew I needed to protect both myself and my sons. I had visions of what could happen in the future as they got older. What if my son had stabbed him? What if he ended up in prison because of him, or worse still, what if my sons were left without a mother? That was it, that unconditional love you have for your children, the thoughts of them growing up without me gave me that courage, that strength to stick with my decision.

That final slap across the face. It was a few weeks after that horrifying incident with my son. I arrived back home late. You see, I would be given a curfew, if I was out. Standing in the bedroom he backed me into a corner, questioning me, "Why were you late? Who were you with?", the usual interrogation. I just stood there, saying nothing, just nodding my head, he hated that. He'd prefer me to answer back so that would be his excuse for hitting me. Then wallop, full force slap across the face. Well let me tell you, all that rage and anger erupted inside of me, that image of my son standing up to him flashed in my mind, I stepped away from the corner, looked him straight in the eye and I promised him that he would never lay a hand on me again and I walked out of the bedroom. He never touched me again.

Now it certainly wasn't plain sailing from that moment, it took me another two years before I finally managed to get him out of the house. You see, in his eyes he had every right to live with his son. He made constant threats to take my son and said that I would never see him again. He was African, he could return to Africa and disappear with my son never to be found. It was a very difficult time, he would try to play on my emotions, getting me to almost feel sorry for him. I had his family in Africa pleading with me to give him another chance, he would cry and beg me not to end it and at times I would almost feel sorry for him, but I kept telling myself NO, you made that final decision you need to stick with it. Think of your children, your own sanity for goodness sake. My sitting room became my bedroom. I continued with my studies but at weekends I just wanted to be out of the house. I would take the kids and just go to friends' houses, relying too much on alcohol just to forget everything for a few hours. I remember drinking with my brother one night, I just fell to pieces, lost it, constantly crying, I just couldn't stop. He had enough of listening to me about the situation and told me that I needed to be strong, he was just going to change the locks and that would be the end of that.

The locks changed, new key in my hand, I had an overwhelming sense of victory, 'You did it, girl!' I thought to myself. But let me tell you, it sure as hell was no easy ride, there was no way he was going to give up that easily. My boys were safe, they were staying with my sister that night. My heart racing, full of fear when I heard him try to open the door that night. My hands were trembling as I sent that very last message telling him that I no longer wanted him in my life. Following that, he made phone call after phone call with numerous threats through voice and text messages, I replied to none of them. I just had my phone on silent and sat in darkness. He sat outside my house in his car for what seemed like forever. The next day I went down to the police station and explained the situation and that I might need their assistance to get him out of the house, if I let him in to take his belongings, because I knew that only then would he have no excuse to manipulate his way back into the house. I went into my neighbour's house and waited for him to take his stuff out. I'm laughing to myself now as I write this because when I came back to the house after he had left, he had taken most of his belongings but he still thought he was getting the last laugh, taking things like the iron, even down to taking all my clothes and shoes because he had paid for them, like seriously I ask, How sad is that? I sure as hell didn't care, I would be happier walking around in a black bag knowing that I was finally free from him. The first thing I did was buy new pillows, duvet and bed linen. It was the best night sleep I had in twelve years. The threats continued, and he tried his best to intimidate me, but I was determined this time that he wouldn't win.

Little by little, I was taking back control. I had one more year left on my VTOS course and I was encouraged to apply for a degree course to continue with my education and then hopefully back into employment, finally get myself a career and feel like I had a purpose. But let's not forget, I had just broken free from twelve years of being controlled, emotionally and physically abused. I honestly think, when it comes down to it, an abusive relationship leaves you with two choices: either to be the real you, true to yourself and authentic or be who you think your abuser wants you to be, the latter being the one that keeps you in the cycle of abuse and the cycle of abusing your Self. For the next eighteen months or so, I chose that second choice. My first rebellious thoughts were to go out when I wanted, with who I wanted. I was single, and he certainly didn't control me anymore! By day, I tried to be normal, being a mother, focusing on studying, the new challenge of starting college and of course the gym. But I was partying at the weekends, binging on alcohol, ending up at house parties and snorting lines of cocaine, loving all the attention from younger guys. I used to love their reaction when I told them I had two teenage sons. I started hanging out with a younger guy, he was twenty-six, I was thirty-eight. He had a lot of his own problems but for some reason I was a sucker for his sad stories. I enjoyed the flirting between us, yet again another charmer. You can see the pattern unfold again, right? One night after another binge on alcohol and cocaine, well let's just say the inevitable happened and we ended up in bed together. Certainly not the happy ever after. Another toxic relationship but the difference this time is that I was the abuser. I was allowing myself to be emotionally messed up, I was the one abusing myself binging on alcohol and cocaine.

I was spiralling into self-destruct mode. All that hurt, pain and anger took over, angry at myself, angry with the world, angry with life. I was spending way too much time and energy on people that sure as hell where not adding any value to my life. Chasing around after the guy I was seeing, trying to fix him and solve his problems, but always running away from myself and running away from the problems I was having closer to home. My eldest son was going through a really tough time too and where was I when he needed me the most? They were very testing times and my relationship with him was chaotic. I had no control over me, so how was I going to have control over him? I don't know how I survived that first year of college, but somehow, that strength of character within me, that something at the core of my being, and that one passion and positive thing throughout all those obstacles in my life, apart from my kids, was the gym.

December 2012 was the turning point for me. The younger guy had traded me in for a younger model. I was hurting so badly, not because of heartbreak, but because I had come to the realisation that I had yet again been living a lie. Lying on my bed in the darkness, I just broke down. I knew there and then I had to decide, either I stay here, stuck, wallowing in self-pity or I find the courage to change. I knew that I had to learn to love me, I needed to heal and rebuild the relationship I had with myself. I needed to nourish my mind, body and spirit. And I was willing to do it.

I now understand that when you are willing to change, it's a time for releasing old beliefs and learning new ones. Fear is a major factor when it comes to change, but I know what it's like to feel fear, I've been there. Being honest with yourself will hurt, you might not like yourself at times for past mistakes, but honestly, you need to let go of all that and forgive yourself. Beating yourself up only keeps you stuck. Live your life for you. There will always be tough decisions, you may need to distance yourself from friends, even family to protect yourself from toxic environments, for example. Have the courage to break free, if a situation doesn't serve you. Don't be a slave to an environment, your energy does not need to be wasted, keep that energy to build YOU up. Decide who you want to become. Be the best version of yourself and create that drama-free lifestyle you deserve. Forget the shame and fear of being judged because when you start sending out different vibes to the world, you will no longer attract judgemental people, only people who will listen, empathise and give you a sense of victory, victory for breaking free from those barriers that prevented you from being the real you. Don't ever feel ashamed, those that judge you are not worth your time and they certainly are not paying you rent to live in your headspace. Get rid!

It's been a long, long road with plenty of obstacles, I still make mistakes, I still get days where my past comes back to haunt me, but for every obstacle I have learnt a valuable lesson, and each lesson has continued to make me stronger. I have worked so hard on ME over the last six years and continue to work on myself each day, I know now that I AM ENOUGH, even with all my past mistakes. I put my head down and focused on me, working from the inside out, I did what was best for me.

You've got to start believing in yourself, you can do anything you want to do. I did! I graduated in September 2014 at forty-one with a second-class double honours degree in modern languages, French and Spanish. I still got knock backs after graduating, not getting jobs I applied for etc., but all those No's kept pushing me into finding my true purpose in life. I enrolled on a Nutrition course and got my Personal Trainer certification.

There is nothing like that feeling, that Phoenix rising from the ashes, and that's exactly how I felt stepping out on stage in my first ever Bodybuilding competition. Forty-three years young, in a bikini, looking like I'd been tangoed, I was full of fear, but the difference this time was that this kind of fear was a positive kind, I was a better version of me. I felt strong and confident. I felt empowered.

I decided to turn that passion for health and fitness into a living. Of course, the fear factor set in, but I took the plunge and set up my own business in the community centre where I first took the step in finding my true self. Apart from my boys, 'GYM' has been the one man that has enhanced my life and given me the confidence and strength to carry on and be me, even in times where life seemed not worth it. I now want to empower others to be the healthiest, happiest version of themselves, through self-care, positive mindset, feeding our bodies with nutritious foods, physical activity, creating a lifestyle that helps you live and be the best version of yourself.

So, ask yourself these questions right now: Are you being true to yourself? I want you to take some time and think about it, look at your environments, whether it be in the workplace, at home, a relationship or friends. Are you where you want to be or are you living in other people's comfort zones, living a lie? Are you living your best life, being the best version of yourself? If not, start by seeking from within, stop reaching outside of yourself looking for other people to save you, because only you have the power to save yourself. Find your inner peace and your authentic self will learn to appreciate your strengths and accept your weaknesses. Your life will be bliss because YOU decided who YOU wanted to become. It's our ability to respond to life, not in a victim way, but in a way that empowers us. And trust me when I tell you, it's the best feeling ever when you don't have to be dependent on an outside person, outside validation and to know that YOU have tremendous abilities to make positive changes in your life and the lives of others.

Now, with my youngest son just turning eighteen and my eldest son a dad himself, I think it's finally time for me to allow the universe to connect me with that someone special. I have nurtured that self-love and I am ready now to embark on the next chapter of my life finding that someone special who will add that something extra to my life.

Respect and Self-Worth
by Lucy Carty

Let's get this straight from the get-go, you deserve respect! We all do, and we are worthy of it. As you read through my chapter, you will begin to understand why respecting, valuing and loving yourself is the most important gift you can give yourself. It's no coincidence that I get to write this chapter a few weeks after the passing of legend soul singer, Aretha Franklin. "R-E-S-P-E-C-T find out what it means to me…" is the main line of the song. When I belt this tune out loud and sing those words, I immediately feel empowered. Here's the thing, respect begins with you, my friend. You need to respect yourself, start where you are. Understand that no one will value you, if you cannot even value and respect yourself.

In my chapter I want to empower you with the gift of valuing and respecting yourself, and I promise, it will feel amazing, so much so that when you begin respecting and valuing yourself more, you will see an immediate shift in your life and it will all be good. I truly respect that you have taken the time to stop and read my chapter, which I hope you will come back to and read over and over, if you ever lose your way, which can sometimes happen too!

I don't come from a place of great academia or possess any formal psychology qualification, but I want to share with you what I know about respect and how my life experiences have taught me the importance of respecting and valuing myself. I would not be taking part in this book, if I hadn't put value on what I want to share with you, and if I hadn't respected and loved myself to make it to this level. So yes, I am a classic case of someone who, after many years, has finally got the concept of truly loving, respecting and valuing myself.

I was raised on a farm in the West of Ireland, the youngest of two girls. Both of us were adopted but not biological sisters. That's a story for another day but I may touch on it briefly in this chapter. Given that my sister and I had no brothers, we had to get stuck in and help on the farm. Although I moaned and gave out about it then, looking back it was a brilliant upbringing, being shown to respect nature. Farm life wasn't idyllic but it's the fondest memories that stay with me and the not so nice that I credit to shaping me today. My father, the lord rest him, was a silent hardworking man and highly respected in the community. A simple man, his work ethos spoke for itself. He was always positive and smiling. He read the paper every day, went for a pint in his local pub every night and knelt beside his bed every morning to say his prayers.

My mother was the matriarch and disciplinarian in the family, a force to be reckoned with, even now in her ninety-first year (oh boy she won't appreciate me telling you her age!). She ruled all and my father was happy to let her do so. As a child you don't fully understand the dynamics of your parents' relationship. I never saw public displays of affection or cards, flowers or great declarations of love, but I saw two friends who worked side by side every day and shared a deep love and respect for one another, something that dictated the destiny of my relationships in the following years.

The Importance of Respect

Respect and self-worth are so important that they are even listed in *Maslow's Hierarchy of Needs*. You may or may not be familiar with the works of Abraham Maslow but back in the 1940s he spoke about human needs. The basics included things like food and shelter, and he expanded right out to the concept of self-actualization, i.e. being all that you can be.

And what do ya know, right up there is Self-Esteem/RESPECT/Status/Recognition! Respecting yourself is an essential need, not just something that would be nice to have, it is essential to your happiness and empowerment. And respect starts with you, respecting your body and mind.

Think of your most precious possession for a moment. How do you care for it? Maybe it's your dog, for example. You walk them, groom them, give them lots of attention and cuddles, get them a little toy or treat now and again, or maybe it's your car. You get it serviced, put the best fuel in it, get it valeted, waxed and washed regularly etc. It might be a piece of jewellery with sentiment attached, it's kept in a velvet box and only worn on special occasions. (If it's a person I'll be covering respect and relationships further on in my chapter. That'll be fun!) These are all examples of how you show respect for things outside of ourselves, BUT do you place that much respect and care on yourself? Do you neglect what's important to you in any way? I hope you are making a connection here. For the purposes of demonstrating an important point, I would like you to do a little exercise right now. I want you to find a mirror and when you have the mirror, look at yourself. That person looking back at you is the most precious thing right now. That person has value and deserves love and respect. Once that person is cared for and respected, everything else falls into place.

Personally, I look in the mirror some days and I think, "Dear God!", if I see a wrinkle, a fold of fat, a grey rib of hair (or a hundred) and other days, since I've started this journey, I've started saying "Thank you God. I'm here, I'm healthy and loving the person looking back at me." Those days are steadily increasing. It takes practice, but you just need to see one thing and build on that.

Respect your body. Mind it like your most prized possession. Feed it good healthy food, let it rest, let it move, laugh, love and be thankful. By the law of averages, I have lived over half my life and, although I have taken the "scenic" route through life, it has gone so fast! I've spent so long berating myself about my flaws and letting others disrespect me because I didn't think I was good enough. Now every day is spent working on loving myself and respecting myself, not in a narcissistic way, but in a kind, loving way. That said, it is totally okay to strut down the street now and then like John Travolta, with *Staying Alive* playing in your head, because you got this!

Respect and Intuition

So, how do you know if you're being disrespected? Well, you just know. You know, if something feels right or wrong. It may be what was said, or not said, a deed, a look that made you feel like, well, basically shit, it hurt, it may have made you feel angry or worthless. By the time you have finished my chapter you will be impervious (remember that word!) to attempts to disrespect you and you will RISE above them. Occasionally, you may have to call someone out on their behaviour towards you, but you will be doing it calmly and in a dignified manner from now on. Too many people have become sick or even ended their lives because of their inability to prevent someone else disrespecting them and undermining them. I will show you how I have dealt with incidences where I had been disrespected and how I coped.

"Respect Radar"

The wonderful Donna Kennedy refers to our brains being like a smartphone and that we download various apps (information programmes) from our app store (our environment) into our phone (our brain). When these apps are downloaded, opened, engaged, and used often enough, the programme becomes so familiar to us that we could almost use it in our sleep. In real terms, we can see this in learning a language, learning to read, creating habits, behaviours and even talents that we acquire as we go through life, sometimes with associated emotions. We start with a basic template and get more advanced as we add to it and practice it.

Now let's imagine that the app store has brought out a new app called the *Respect Radar.* Visualize it, for a moment. Imagine being in a situation where the app is opened, during an incidence of disrespect, for example. Let's say someone says or does something disrespectful to you. Ordinarily you might automatically retaliate to what was said or done because that's how you've always reacted. But instead of reacting, what if you became intentionally aware of that Respect Radar app in your brain, and instead of reacting you pause. Just like an app on a smart phone, just because it is opened doesn't mean you have to keep it open or engage with it! In that pause moment, ask yourself, 'Is this behaviour or comment high or low on my radar?', followed by 'Do I need to engage it or close it down?' Slowing it down and being conscious of the activity of that app means you have a choice to engage or close it down. We live in an age when people are offended and triggered in ludicrous proportions by others' comments. For example, social media can quickly "blow up" in response to a new PC term being used or not used, some terms long overdue and some, well, plain stupid, in my opinion. Nonetheless, people respond, often with huge emotion.

I have learned to understand my "Respect Radar" and how to use it productively. I suggest you consider it and take a moment to download it in your mind. It's a brilliant tool and you are the master of it. As you begin to value yourself and respect yourself more and set those boundaries, your Respect Radar app won't go into emotional overdrive. It will sit there and be used productively when needed. Again, imagine what your Respect Radar app might look like. See it as an app that displays on a phone, that little coloured button. Then think of it containing all the following information and lessons in this chapter. Once you have the information and lessons, practice often!

Realise your self-worth!

My first true lesson about sticking up for myself and realising my self-worth happened over twenty years ago. I had just started work in our local hospital as a Nurse on temporary contract.

Back then Matrons ruled with iron fists and were authoritarian figures to the point of bullying, in some instances, and if you were junior staff, which I was, you didn't rank very high on the Respect

Radar. I had called into the staff wages office with some issue or other, to be met with the Matron who literally lambasted me in front of the whole office. What did I think I was doing "annoying senior staff, GET BACK to work immediately." I left with my tail between my legs, embarrassed and feeling quite small. I literally could do no good for the rest of the day, I was so upset. I was living at home at the time and of course my mother picked up that I was hurt, so I told her what happened. I got the classic "Well, if I were you" line, as mothers do, and normally I'd zone out, as daughters do. This time her advice was gold "You need to speak to this woman" advised my mother "What she did was highly disrespectful, you are a fully qualified Nurse and as good, if not better, than anyone else in there. She had no right to speak to you that way." I thought my mother was nuts because, if I dared to even speak to Matron, she could breathe fire onto me and I'd be reduced to a crisp. My mother continued, "If you let her away with speaking to you like this, she will think she can speak to you like this always. You have to face this. Ring her now and sort it." My mother was and is a courageous woman with an innate capacity to recognize bullshit and say it like it is. No one, but no one, would dare disrespect her, so perhaps a little of that courage rubbed off onto me, although back then I was not feeling it.

Really, I just wanted to roll into a ball and self-soothe until it all went away, but I knew deep down that she was totally right, and it had to be sorted. With trembling knees and hands, I picked up the phone and dialled her office, my voice trembling. I asked to speak with her.

"Yes?", she answered. I wanted to slam down the phone there ad then. Instead, I started to speak, my mouth dry and trembling.

"I...want to speak to you about the incident today where you spoke to me in such a curt manner in front of other members of staff. I was very embarrassed, I was on my break and I am entitled to query an issue with my wages." I just blurted it out in one breath.

I was met with silence. No doubt her chest filled with indignation and her head did a 360 with the insolence that a lowly member of staff would dare call her office, let alone call her out on her rudeness. The blood pounded in my ears, but I went on.

"I felt it unnecessary to have been spoken to in that way." Courage began slowly coursing through my veins, "And I expect an apology."

(Dear God, I am SO fired)

"I am a member of staff and I'm sure there is no need to get the Union involved over this incident."

(GO LUCY!!...where did that come from? Now you are worse than fired ...you are now DEAD)

Silence...then...

"Well, I am truly sorry you felt that way and I apologise for the incident", she said.

Excuse my French, but I nearly fucking died! Did I actually hear this correctly?

She continued, "I accept your apology and we will speak no more of it."

BOOM!!!

Dear God, I didn't die, burst into flames or get fired. I stuck up for my rights, calmly, and without aggression. I showed her respect, in that I didn't insult her and yet I got my point across. It was one of the most empowering moments of my life. It was a defining moment, all thanks to my mother.

From then on, if I felt a blip at all on my *Respect Radar,* I took a moment to analyse it, if I needed to nip the disrespect in the bud or ignore and continue living my life. Believe it or not, I enjoyed a respectful relationship (okay she'd nod at me, but hey!) with my boss from there on in.

Know your boundaries and set boundaries

Boundaries are key to your happiness and empowerment, and if you don't know how to set them, allow me to insert my tuppence worth and, hearing my mother's words "Well if I were you...". I'm assuming you have a home, possibly with a garden. If you don't, imagine you have a lovely white picket fence around your beautiful home and garden. If you live in the countryside, imagine that a herd of cattle broke into your property, smashed your fence and trampled your garden or, for city dwellers, someone has just dumped their trash over your fence. How would that make you feel? Is it okay? Would you be enraged that someone dared to defile your property? Well, it's no different when it comes to you and your happiness. Don't let anyone else trample on your mind or chuck stuff in your personal space. Someone may be using you as a trampling ground for their issues, someone may be dumping all their psychological trash on you or they may be physically in your space. But you know deep down in your gut that it is not okay, and your *Respect Radar* is alarming all over the place. Value your psychological property!

In the early years of 2000 I was a separated mother of two small boys. I had emerged from a tumultuous marriage and was feeling vulnerable. I had people very kind and genuinely supportive and I had others pretending to be. My parenting skills and life choices were questioned, and advice was coming from all ends, because

I wasn't in a place of valuing myself or placing boundaries. I let those people hop the fence and have a walk all over my garden, so to speak. I even had another parent (a man) think it okay to chastise my child in front of me. No, I wasn't rearing an angel, but my *Respect Radar* was pinging all over the place with that incident, it was totally inappropriate.

I dated on and off (Total Floozie, be more in her line to mind to stay at home and mind her kids). I was damned, if I did, and damned, if I didn't, by others' standards, no matter what I did, so you see, I had all sorts of rubbish chucked over my wall and the gates to my psychological property swinging open for all to come in and have a look around.

Reconnecting with my biological family had a major impact. As previously mentioned, I am an adopted person. Maybe the makings of another book, but the gist of the story is thus…

My parents were young when they discovered they were pregnant with me. Even though they were engaged to be married, in 1970 you just DID NOT have a child out of wedlock and so I was adopted. They married the year after and went on to have five more children. Some would say how terrible, but you cannot un-ring a bell. I had a wonderful upbringing with wonderful parents and I'd like to think I'm a happy blend of genetics and upbringing. Unfortunately, I never met my biological mother as she died at the very young age of thirty-five, leaving my father to rear my five siblings. I will never know her story or version of events, but I know this, my father loved my mother deeply and still does to this day. Knowing that I was conceived by two people in love was consoling to me and healing even. I slowly came to appreciate the life I had with two wonderful sets of parents. I learned to value myself once again and reclaim my boundaries.

I began to parent my own children and be present, owning my psychological property. One person remarked to my older son, who was twelve at the time, "Oh you're the man of the house now." I corrected him and told him that I WAS the man of my own house. No child should have that title thrust upon them, I was the head of the household and firmly in the driving seat, not perfect, only human, but doing unapologetically it in the best way I knew how. And sometimes one parent doing a good job is sometimes better than two doing a half-baked job. My *Respect Radar* app was on red alert for some time, as I had to re-educate people on how my life and my choices were absolutely none of their business, and this was done by establishing clear boundaries.

Understand Relationships

I've had two defining relationships in my life so far. My first was with my son's father, to whom I was married. He was my first love or whatever one is capable of at eighteen years of age. My mother used to say, "You should respect yourself like Our Virgin Mary", to which my eyes would roll or glaze over. My ex-husband was extremely handsome, and I could not believe he fancied me, or even paid me attention. I was shy around boys and a shitty mingler. I couldn't flirt like the other girls. I wasn't cool or popular. I was Bridget Jones but much more verbally clumsy. When this Adonis shone his attention upon me ...'Sod that advice Mammy, I got me a boyfriend!' Our problem was we were not friends. We looked good together and we had a circle of friends. I was delighted. I had a boyfriend and then a husband...oh joy! How socially acceptable was?! And validated as a real person, because I'm married!

We fought bitterly, and in most instances, I would give in for a quiet life. I was determined to keep up the facade, but It was soul destroying. I could gradually see that I wanted more from life than him, and his way of keeping me in my place seemed to be to verbally and psychologically abuse me. The rows and personal attacks were horrible. In my opinion, he was a bully. My friends stayed away. Most social occasions would be a nightmare where he would kick off and ruin the evening. I was nothing but an "Arse wiper" (my nursing career), a "Half Breed" and a "Bastard" (alluding to my adoption status), and when I suggested counselling sure it was "all in my head" and when you hear it often enough, you begin to believe it.

My light bulb moment came when there was the usual ding-dong going on and my eldest son, who was then three years old, walked between us and said to him "DON'T SHOUT AT MY MAMMY!" My heart broke that my beautiful boy had to see the wrong that I had accepted for so long. I made up my mind there and then that this was not a life that I wanted for my children. I wanted them to see a loving relationship, not a toxic one for them to accept as normal and influence their future relationships. Do I lay the blame squarely at my ex-husband's feet? No, as there was a lot of immaturity on both sides. Looking back now, I see that he came into our relationship knowing what he knew and accepting it as normal. I didn't know how to value myself and putting up with it was not a good mix. However, I am delighted to say it gave me the most precious gift of all in my life, my two sons. They are kind, thoughtful, funny men who know themselves and are compassionate grounded people. Would they have been different people if I had remained in the marriage? Yes, I believe so. After all those years, my ex and I divorced, and a divorce party was mentioned. I knocked the suggestion on the head totally. I have no regrets about my marriage, as it has shaped me and would be totally disrespectful to the two lives we created.

My second relationship was totally different. I was set up on a blind date by friends. I was struck by his kindness and sense of fun. He had come out of a terrible marriage also and I guess we found comfort in each other and sharing our stories. He was the total opposite to what I had experienced. I was treated like a queen, so much so that I had to pinch myself at times. He supported and respected me, and it was like a warm security blanket around me. I loved it and loved him. We shared a great sense of humour, talked and travelled together enjoying new adventures. He adored me and I him. His family welcomed me, he was a wonderful role model for my boys, showing them how to treat a woman with respect. I do think they were reassured to see their mother happy and being cared for by a good man.

So, what happened? I changed jobs, I moved from working as a nurse in a hospital to the private industry and eventually opened my own business, *Eden Skin and Laser Clinic*, with his total and full support…and then I changed. I became driven and ambitious, wanting to achieve more and, as he said in his own words, "I couldn't follow you." Our relationship paid the price for my drive and success. The cracks came ever so subtly, a remark, a snip, a mood, silences…I could not stand by and watch the relationship disintegrate into a place of total resentment. I loved him and respected him enough to realise that this good man needed to be loved fully as a human being, not half loved by me. I also realised that I too was deserving of love in all its forms for the person I am too. We parted ways and moved on.

I am now contently living a single life, although I joke that I may have one or two more marriages left in me. I am, for now, concentrating on my most precious relationship of all, the relationship with myself. Discovering what I love and loving myself by working on nurturing my mind, body and spirit. And from time to time I dabble in the dating scene but armed with my standards and, if he can't see my worth, that's okay as there's someone for everyone. But it is not stopping me from living my best life. Now, if George Clooney happens to leave his uber intelligent beautiful wife and happy home and wants to trade up for a menopausal half-mad woman from the west of Ireland, then yes, I'll try to clear a window for him.

Recognise Biddies and Bullies

Just for fun I want to touch on these two entities. They are unfortunate creatures and are to be found in almost every aspect of your life. It's good to be able to recognise them! I don't want to dwell on them too much, as it's just important for you to realise this breed of person has zero power over you. In fact, you may find their behaviour rather amusing and you may even have empathy for them. If you have your *Respect Radar* turned on, you will pick up on their shenanigans. They may be cleverly disguised as a friend, a co-worker, a family member even!

Biddies are especially common, and I have coined the term where a group of Biddies come together as "Idiom". When I think of Biddydom, I think of the scene from the movie *The Snapper,* where a gaggle of women congregate across the road from the Curley household. Squeezing out whines of disapproval from their tightly folded arms like badly played bagpipes.

Bullies are particularly hideous beings also. But are they? Unfortunately, they are to be pitied, as they are coming from a place of suffering and have nowhere to go with it? In my opinion, they are carrying self-doubt, insecurity and lack of respect and value for themselves. Your attention and response are their oxygen and they feed on it only to throw more at you. They are not worth your while, their small mindedness and tactics are powerless. Ignoring them is like throwing water on the Wicked Witch of the West. (*Wizard of Oz*) They simply melt and vanish from your Respect Radar. So, you see, these people have to be pitied more than despised. However, they ain't your puppy to rescue and taking notice of their words and deeds only eats into your happy time where you are too busy valuing and respecting yourself.

Is it too late to get respect?

My friend is it NEVER ever too late for you respect yourself, and command respect from others.

You may have lived a life of unhappiness, without love or respect shown to you. You are already envisioning a Biddy or a Bully that is making your life hell right now, and you are realising that "I've wasted so much time heeding this eejit!" Start with building those boundaries, stop the invaders of your head space. Sometimes it may involve you summoning up the courage to face them and say, "Hang on, this is not acceptable", perhaps a gentle reminder is all people need to see that you are a human worthy of respect. A boss, a co-worker, a friend, a family member or a lover may need to be told to simply back TF off over your boundaries, as they may have unwittingly over-stepped it. And when you are coming from a place of loving and valuing yourself, others will see that and respect you all the more for it and all will be well.

This may be not possible for now as your invader may be particularly persistent in their disrespect of you, so start simple. I was given a brilliant tip from a wonderful lady recently. Write that person's name on a piece of paper, fold it up and put it in your freezer! You are literally freezing their vibe towards you and freezing them out of your life for now. How powerful is that?!

The Scale of Disrespect

Disrespect comes in many forms and levels. For example, on an extreme level disrespect might be being physically hurt or at a risk of physical or psychological harm. If that's the case, get out now! Tell a friend or confide in someone you trust. Being hurt is not the life you were meant to lead. No one should have that power over your destiny or your life. You have choices. You always have choices. Find another circle to socialize in. Take the time to work on YOU.

When I went on to open my own business, I felt the vibe of surprise, envy and incredulities from some, in that I had even dared to do such a thing. "You've changed", was a remark passed, no doubt to keep me in my place and suppress any notion of bettering myself to keep that insecure person happy. Sometimes a big sign is a big target and I've no doubt that I have my critics and detractors, but having reviewed it, guess what? What people think of me is none of my business! My priority is valuing myself, being a kickass mother, providing a professional service in my clinic and living my best life. I have closed the gates shut tight to my psychological property and, inside it is all about continuously striving to raise my frequency and be around like-minded people and be happy. That's it!

I AM

And so, my beautiful worthy friend, I hope you now realise that you are deserving of love and respect. Respect is your God given right and your gift from the universe. I have many more life shaping incidences where I had to growl a bit over the boundary fence at a few trespassers, I think you generally get the picture. I am leaving you with this fantastic exercise that I do most mornings on my daily commute to work. For far too long I listened to the tune "I am fat, I am ugly, I am unlovable, I am stupid, I am not worthy." Ah you've probably heard that too? Isn't it a shit song? It'll never get to No.1! Instead rewrite that tune with positive affirmations. Here are some of mine.

I am Brave

I am Happy

I am Free

I am Beautiful

I am where I need to be right now

I am worthy

Make your own list now

I am _____

I am_____

I am_____

I am_____

I am_____

I am_____

I am_____

I am_____

I am_____

Start with anything, as long as it's positive.

And yes, on occasion if you have a terrible day, the tune may change temporarily to the negative. If that happens, picture your inner Simon Cowell, and picture him rolling his eyes at that pitiful tune and saying, "THAT was AWFUL!"

Much love and respect to you, my friend. I hope you enjoy the rest of the book written by some pretty amazing ladies, which I have been fortunate to collaborate with and I hope you will be inspired and empowered by all our messages.

Namaste.

Lucy

Loving yourself
by Jenny McSweeney

Let me tell you how one small event impacted my choices around both finding love and ultimately loving myself.

This is so hard because in order for me to share all this with you, I have to face up to the fact that I'm not a shit individual. I have to step away from everything bad I've ever believed or was led to believe about myself and embrace the facts that are in front of me which are that I am the very opposite of everything I ever believed. I'm more comfortable, as many of us are, staying in the negative space where we listen to our internal dialogue, so to step out of this space and compliment myself for all I have achieved and start loving myself for all the greatness that I am because the facts can't be denied, I had to leave my old story and step into my new story .

Can you remember the excitement you felt starting "Big School"? Well I was no different. I was a very excited four-year-old little girl and I had just received a brand-new pencil. Back then the pencils were already sharpened so mine had the coolest pointiest tip to it. I remember I held it so tight all day from the moment I got it. For those of you who know me I have an abundance of energy and I was no different back then. I was a happy excited little girl even at bedtime.

One particular evening I ran (actually, I probably sprinted) to give my dad a kiss before bed. I ran into the room so fast and while I was focused on getting my hug and kiss all of a sudden there was an angry aggressive roar directed towards me. I froze to the spot in fear. What I didn't realise was the pointed tip of the pencil had gone straight into a vein in his arm.

Up to that point I don't remember ever seeing someone that angry, never mind that angry at me. As any little girl does, I started to cry while my mother helped me to bed. She tried to keep me quiet at the same time. The days and weeks that followed changed everything for me, not that I knew this at the time. I was far too young to understand the emotions I felt. That event resulted in me being afraid of my Dad for a long time and I learned from then that the easiest way to get through life was to be quiet around my dad. It was survival technique even at that young age.

My natural energy then changed when I was near my Dad because my experience had shown me that if I was being me, I would hurt him and if I hurt him, he would get angry with me again. A four-year old's mentality became my new story of what I believed to be the truth about life and people, and the last thing I wanted to do was hurt anyone or make them angry. I became very aware that even when my friends came home from school with me, I should pre-warn them that my dad may shout. I always made excuses. Was there any need to do this? My belief said there was, so I did.

I also decided that I would only tell my Dad about any of my achievements, if I knew I'd get a good reaction. Looking back, I don't even think he was aware of the situation I found myself in with him. I never realised how that event had Impacted so my choices in my life from then on. It's almost as if I continued to crave the love that I felt I lost from my Dad that night.

The need for love or more truthfully to be seen and heard by him as I got older turned into a need for validation that would be generalized to others. I craved for people to tell me I was good enough and all this bubbling energy I had was okay too. In an attempt to prove this to at least myself, if not to everyone else, I joined every single class or team that I could. Every day in school I stayed back to do whatever activity was on, some I was good at some I was shocking at I! joined the camogie team (local and school team), badminton (it took me about four months before I actually connected with the shuttlecock), volleyball, which I loved, netball (to be honest it was hit and miss, with the misses being the ball in the net), basketball (my ability to play is dodgy enough to this day) and circuit training. It seemed that the more intense the activity it was physically, the more I loved it. It was a way to release some of that huge energy I had before I got home. I also noticed that I was very reactive to people, if they said anything that may suggest I wasn't good enough.

I am child number six of seven children and even though we were loved in a big way we were never really told it, well not until we were much older anyway, but that was partly a sign of the times. As such, I went in search for love.

I was in serious relationships from the young age of thirteen. I wasn't happy in some relationships, but I would never leave because, if I did, they could get hurt and ultimately get angry with me. At all costs I wanted to avoid feeling unloved. To stop history (the event when I was four) repeating itself I started to suppress what I felt, but I needed validation from someone, specifically male, to love me. The little girl once again was looking for approval, but these decisions were to be at the cost of my own happiness, which I was later to find out.

Up until a couple of years ago I would avoid confrontation at all costs. Let's say if someone crossed what I now know to be my boundary, I avoided saying anything, so I didn't have to deal with any uncomfortable feelings. On the flip side of this, the suppressed feelings would build and eventually explode in the wrong way and of course always at the wrong time, even sometimes at the wrong person. That reactive behavior I noticed at a young age was just getting a personality of its own because I wasn't dealing with it. I didn't even realize I had to deal with it. It was just the way I was, so everyone could like it or lump it, So the question I asked myself was, 'What was I afraid of? What did I think would happen?' Well I suppose if you're calling someone on their bulls**t, you need to have a kind of self-confidence, which I now know I didn't have. Did I look confident? I absolutely did but it was all a front to disguise how I was really feeling or who I really was and if I'm to be perfectly honest, I didn't want them to think I wasn't a nice person. Oh, did I have a lot to learn! Being nice isn't about taking crap from people, being nice is essentially about being nice to yourself or loving yourself.

My search (that I didn't realise I was on) continued until I found a man that absolutely showered me with love, affection, attention and gifts - you name it, I got it. He put me on a pedestal that I never asked for but at the time I lapped it up and loved every minute of all this fantastic attention. At different times in our lives we need different things and for me the timing of this was absolutely perfect. It surely meant that I was lovable, right? How could it mean anything else? Checklist - I felt amazing. I was needed. I felt loved. Surely everything was perfect, and that void was filled. 'Eeeeh...no, because the love was coming from someone other than me. Hold on now, I don't need to love me I just need to love everyone else! Isn't that what makes them love me back? If I give everyone enough love then that fixes everything, right?!', I thought.

This made me feel great but disempowered me from loving myself. It clouded over the real issue and, with my rose-tinted glasses on I was not going to see or understand what was going on. This huge security blanket disguised my lack of love for myself, which as I've said before, was my biggest life lesson to date. What happens when you get showered with so much love, attention and everything you've ever dreamed of? Well, I'll tell you. It becomes a huge problem when it stops coming in the huge waves that it initially came from. I was again on a search for love, but this time unconsciously. What kind of a lunatic searches for love unconsciously? The sort of person that doesn't love themselves. The sort of person that doesn't really know what's wrong in their lives or that there even is something wrong. I was unhappy but chose to ignore the fact.

I was in my mid-thirties and alone, well alone is a bit harsh statement, because I had a beautiful daughter and a loving family around me, but that wasn't what I was seeking. I had an advantage though. I was blessed with a growth mindset and even in my lowest darkest days, and let me tell you they were low and dark, I had a tool that I used, which was my smile and my energy, even though my energy was fake and it drained the life and soul out of me because I was running on empty. It's safe to say at the time I didn't realise that this would ultimately save me and turn my life around. I started reading personal growth books and I read each book three to four times just to keep me focused on something other than the darkness.

This is where the plot twist happened. I got the opportunity to take over the business that I had worked in for twelve years. It would either send me down a darker path or save me. Once again without realising I had a new love, which was achieving my goals. Goal after goal after goal, seeking praise after each achievement, just to fill that void. I craved the attention that the little girl with all that energy, the energy that she was afraid to show, would prove herself through goal setting and goal achieving.

Hold up there now because when I say goals, I don't mean small goals. I mean big goals and "mad ideas", the kind that evoke a response like "Have you got your head in the clouds girl?", but I was focused, determined and driven, like no one you've ever seen before. Surely, I'd be loved, if I achieve "This, That and The Other". I was like a toddler looking for attention. "Look at me. Look what I'm doing now. Aren't I great?!" People started to notice. They started to stop me and congratulate me. That's good, right? I suppose for my ego it was but there was something missing. I was still searching for validation that I am enough, even though I didn't really know what good enough meant. Every fiber of my being was screaming 'Someone please give me the answer!'. I knew they couldn't give it to me. I had to find it in myself and love myself first within the void I felt. It is only now that I know the vastness of that void.

At the time my friends said things like, "You've never not achieved a goal you've set" and they were right. I was so focused that I just went from goal to goal. Not appreciating, not being grateful, just looking for validation all the time to fill that void.

Then, noticing how people perceived me as an achiever, the statement "I'm Amazing" was born. It became the thing to say when I spoke about myself and it became the thing my friends said when they spoke of me, but I didn't believe it and here's the reason why.

At the time I was in a new relationship. It was all beautiful, fuzzy and perfect just as new relationships are, but I was soon to learn that this man was hugely manipulative. I am the polar opposite of a manipulator. I came into the relationship quite vulnerable (I didn't realize this at the time) and when you are vulnerable, you can become a victim very easily. I started to see changes in his behavior towards me, he started accusing me of things that made no sense to me. It involved name calling, which I wasn't used to. It was also controlling behavior, questioning what I did all the time etc. I got used to this because I was terrified to go back to that feeling of being alone. Being alone was far too dark a place for me to even contemplate going back to, so I put up with this new way of being and when I knew I should speak up for myself, I kept quiet.

In no time at all, the relationship we had went from nice to nasty and for most of it I was very confused. I never knew when the next accusation or the next lash of name calling would come. I felt worthless, sad and lonely. 'Why was I so paralyzed that I couldn't fight back?' The confident goal achiever looked perfect on the outside because of those magical tools I told you about earlier, my smile and my energy, no one really saw the true effect that the relationship was having on me. My persona was fake and forced. Inside I was crumbling, I was a mess. The void I was so convinced this relationship would fix got bigger and bigger. I felt the Jenny that everyone loved was slipping away. My gut was screaming but I felt this was the love I deserved.

I believe everything happens to us for a reason and even though I said earlier there was a plot twist, this is the time that everything started to turn and bring me to where I am right now to write this book.

I became friends with a person, who, everyday sent me a video or a quote or a message to put some positivity in my life, to remind me how amazing, loving and kind I really was. This person lifted me up and empowered me to the point where I eventually started to see my worth. Admittedly, it wasn't was easy. In fact, initially I found it hard to even receive the messages and felt embarrassed by them. It took over a year for me to stop resisting the fact that I may be worth loving and not have to be the person who always gave out love.

With my new friend's encouragement, I signed up to do a life coaching course, something I knew I wanted to do for a while but didn't know how to go about it. It was another goal that I absolutely knew I could achieve. As if anyone would even doubt me at this stage! I was unstoppable on the goal achieving front. On October 2017, I walked into a room in The River Lee Hotel in Cork and what I was about to learn, encounter and achieve I would never have predicted. Day 1 was all about Values. 'What the hell are Values?', the chatter started in my head. People started to call out different Values and suddenly I thought, 'Oh, I have them! Respect was definitely my core value. I'm amazing at respecting people. No doubt, I have this in the bag! I'm amazing after all.' Courage was definitely next because I knew how I brought myself back up after being so low, and kindness, yes, kindness because I'm the kindest person in the world. 'Whoohoo this is easy', I was absolutely loving it. The feeling was incredible. I was so glad I was there. Very soon after that we covered Boundaries. Now, beautiful reader, this is where the magic happened. I sat in that classroom for two to three hours and in all over my thirty-nine years before that moment I can honestly say my life never made as much sense as it did then. Every time something was said or explained about boundaries it was like someone was sitting behind me slapping the back of my head. Realization after realization, I was numb...silent...drained...but most importantly I felt so stupid. I know I shouldn't have felt like that but I'm so glad I did because that day has changed my life.

There I was with all my amazing values that I was so very proud of and not a boundary to be seen for miles. I realized that people had been walking all over me and I had let them. I had given them all a free pass. It was like I had a sign on my forehead that said, 'Ah sure I'm fine, don't worry about me, once you're okay'. People had come to expect my kindness and respect it, but they learned that they didn't really need to give it back to me. Why? If I hurt them, they would get angry with me. If they were angry with me, it meant I wasn't loveable. I was nearly forty years old and the little girl was still controlling my life. What kind of BS was this? How could such a small event have this impact on someone's belief system?

It was checklist time again... I've loved ... I've lost...I've read...I've learned …. I've got myself out of the darkness... I've resurrected a business that was failing...I looked manipulation in the eye and rose above it...but now what will I do?

At that point I realised that I need to help that little four-year-old girl. What do I do best? Yes, I achieve goals! I knew it from that moment, this would be the biggest, best, and most impactful goal I would ever set and achieve, and importantly, it would be meaningful. It's funny how belief systems work because as much as I didn't think I was lovable I never doubted my goal achieving. I could fix that little girl.

Setting boundaries was my new mission. It seemed easy and at the beginning but as soon as someone crossed a boundary I had set, I realized it wasn't. It was my biggest test because it meant I had to speak up and confront. 'Confrontation? Nooooo! Suck it up Buttercup, you now *have* to do confrontation.' It was so. Daunting. However, I did it, I spoke up and after I did, I put proper boundaries in place for everyone else I knew and met, one person at a time. I have never in my life seen people exit so fast but the people who left were those that drained my energy, kindness and respect, so they weren't a loss.

My life was finally getting a spring clean which gave me the space to sort other pressing issues in my life. The manipulation relationship had to go. As I've said everything happens for a reason and even though we don't understand everything at the time that they happen it all makes sense at some stage.

With my new understandings and life tools, I decided to improve myself and my life step by step. I don't know why but I knew the first step was to sit and be still, long enough to go back to that little girl who was hurting so much. I just knew if I could help her, everything would start to be better. Ironically, I felt like I was getting close to having a breakdown, which was surreal because I seemed to be in complete control of what was happening and how I was feeling, but I decided it was time to fix things. In order to do this, I needed to be on my own and create the space I needed. I didn't know what or how or anything really at this point only that I needed to be near water. I drove to a beautiful spot and put my feet in the water. As we all know whether there's a heat wave or not in Ireland the water is bloody ankle killing cold, but I stood and closed my eyes and the only thing I remember thinking was, once my ankles stop hurting, I will have connected to the water and that would be my starting point to healing.

I could picture exactly how I looked at age four, my tiny face, big brown eyes, auburn hair tied in a pony tail, sitting at the end of the stairs in my old house. It was the most surreal moment of my life. I knelt in front of this scared little girl who looked at me through huge sad eyes and I put my hands out to hug her. She wrapped her arms around me, and I just whispered 'I have you now. You're safe. I love you.'

I stayed in that space with my eyes closed for quite some time with tears flowing from my eyes. I remember I didn't even get a tissue I just let it flow until it stopped. I never let that little girl go until my tears stopped. I could hear people beside me on that little beach, but I knew I needed to stay with this. That was my moment. That was the moment that I finally knew what self-love was. That was the turning point in my life, and I don't know how but I just knew I had healed a huge part of me that I had expected everyone else to fix for so long. I loved me for me. The giddiness. the energy, everything, absolutely everything. Then, with my eyes still closed, I went on to the next huge hurt I had encountered, and I held that Jenny too. I kept moving forward to each challenging event that had occurred in my life and I hugged each version of myself that had suffered in some way. I just kept loving very part of me that needed it and didn't stop until I came face to face with myself. It was the most breath-taking and scary moment I have ever experienced but it had to happen. The weight of the world lifted from me. I didn't feel better straight away but I just knew in my gut that something incredible had just happened and that it would continue to make a positive impact on me each day.

My life now is very different. It is full of positivity, full of excitement and full of people who are good for my life. I have achieved several things since. I got my life coaching diploma with flying colours and went on to get a distinction in a further QQI level 6 qualification. My business got an award and it is going from strength to strength BUT the big difference in my goal achievements now is that they are all for me, not for validation or gratification from anyone but for me. I still set goals, being part of this book is one of them, but my goals are now achieved for the right reasons and they are taking me in the right direction. I love every bit of my life now and look forward to what lies ahead, with no expectation. I have never felt better than I do now, that my life is in alignment with who I truly am. Now I love myself and I know "I'm Amazing". I feel it in my core.

My amazing father sadly passed away in 2010 but I'm proud and grateful to say he died as my best friend. I wish he could see me now, but I know he's very proud of me. Everything does come right in the end.

So, my friend, my advice to you is this: Go with the flow of life and trust that everything will work out. Question every belief system you have about yourself up to now. Go back as far as you need to and find the source of the belief systems that aren't good for you and change them, you are worthy of love. What's meant for you won't pass you. Without even meeting you, I know you are worthy of happiness and I know you too are AMAZING!

Unleashing the Silent Hero
by Marie Donnery

When I was a young child going to school, I remember most of the basic teaching (Irish, English and Sums) going right over my head, they didn't interest me at all. The things that brought me alive were nursery rhymes, songs, drawing and colouring on paper, knitting, making things with material and being outside playing games with the girls. I loved skipping. We took turns turning the rope and one of us would jump into the centre and skip as we all sang Down in the Valley Where the Green Grass Grows. Piggy Beds was another game that I loved. We made square boxes and numbered them with chalk, one to six. I took many an un-opened tin of shoe polish from our kitchen press. The aim of the game was for us to kick the tin into each box while we hopped on one foot and the first one to make it without losing balance, covering all the six boxes, was the winner.

I remember the morning I made my first holy communion, standing in the kitchen as my Mam dressed me. I can still remember the smell of leather from my new white shoes. They were a gift from my Godmother. I had a beautiful feeling of excitement and goodness inside me, like I was an angel.

When I was eleven years of age, I learned Irish dancing and I loved performing on stage, collecting a few medals and trophies along the way. I also joined a local choir and loved singing, especially when the music teacher asked me to sing solo pieces, it excited me and made me happy. It seemed a natural thing for me to do, especially when I was doing what I loved. I am sure most people that sing or dance feel like that. I realised later in life that it is our natural state to be happy.

When I got older, I left school early and I became a teenage mother at the age of sixteen. This was a huge transition in my life, going from having a childlike mind to being responsible for my beautiful infant. I remember holding my daughter for the first time and feeling an overwhelming love between us. It was unconditional love and pure goodness. It was the same experience with each beautiful baby I had, holding them in my arms for the first time.

My passion for music returned, as my children got older, and I got involved in variety groups and local choirs. I was involved in starting a gospel choir in my local community. While all these things were great to be a part of, I remember looking in the mirror one day and asking myself 'Who am I and what is this life all about?'. I suppose I was in my early thirties then. I was busy rearing a family and yet curious to learn about me, whoever "me" was. I saw an advertisement in the local community centre for a personal development course that was taking place and it was perfect timing for me. This is where my journey of self-discovery began. I loved it and began to learn about myself, as being a young mother and a wife was all I knew, and I guess this was the beginning of finding out who I was and why I was here, so I became hungry to learn more.

The course took place twice a week for twelve weeks and gave me the space to finally think about me, to learn and understand that I was a person and that I had needs. It gave me some great tools to work with, like giving myself permission to take myself out for a day's adventure, or simply soaking in a bath and pampering myself without feeling guilty, or meeting up with friends to talk about adult things, this resulted in me feeling better, looking better and I was better able to cope with the busyness of family life. As my confidence grew, I became even more eager to learn. I went on to do a few follow-on courses that helped me grow and become even more empowered, things like community development leadership, a course that was about learning new skills to have a better understanding and awareness of what people living in communities needed and how to use those skills.

Adult education

I chose to sit for my Junior Certificate exam. It was good to return to education as an adult, as it was my choice to learn, and I obtained a National Vocational Training Award. This was basic knowledge, comprehension and understanding of the English language.

I then enrolled in Steps for Personal Success programme. This course was a key factor and a breakthrough for me, as this is where I learned about my mind and how my thoughts work, namely that what we think we create. Learning that I could control what I was thinking had such a positive impact on me and I knew it could change my life. I felt more empowered and I wanted to share this valuable information with others and show them that things didn't have to stay the way they were, we could simply change our lives by changing our thoughts to more positive thoughts, which has a different impact on the way we live and the results we obtain. In order to do this, I felt I needed to study for a second certificate called Steps in Excellence, which

I did, and this gave me the new skills to deliver the programme. Later I added Facilitation certificates at level 1 and level 2.

The facilitation course was great as it helped me overcome challenges, like speaking out in front of a class, giving a presentation and breaking through lots of fears of the little gremlins (thoughts) that wanted to stop me from moving forward. When the courses finished, I was delighted, and I knew I deserved to have the two certificates. Now I was ready to go to work and take this programme out to wider communities. This was my new passion in life and it excited me. It brought me alive, just as I was excited as a child playing and as a teenager mother experiencing unconditional love.

Whilst on this three-year journey, I met some amazing people, who were looking for change in their own lives, and as I walked with them, it was such a joy and pleasure to watch them grow and share all their experiences with them. I felt privileged and grateful for this.

Career

My career changed direction while working in a local community centre. I saw an opportunity to provide a sandwich service as there was no facilities for people to eat in. I offered to provide fresh sandwiches and beverages at lunch time. One day, on my way home, I noticed a tractor working on a site nearby and I stopped to enquire what was happening. I was informed that there was a development of new homes being built. I heard myself asking the question, 'Who was providing the food for the workers?' I explained to the man I was already making sandwiches for twenty women nearby and would they be interested in this service. I got a resounding yes and the next day I made up breakfast rolls for them. This continued to grow and I was offered my own canteen on the building site, which was where I worked for the next four years, five days a week on site and two days were for preparation while looking after my young family This was hard work and I learned new skills on how to manage a business, cooking, becoming a waitress, stock taking, buying supplies, retailing, cleaning and being a cashier. I never let myself take a day off as I felt so responsible for this new business, but my passion kept me going as I loved this challenge and I loved providing a service, especially on freezing cold days serving lovely hot food as the guys bantered away. They became like my other family.

As the houses were nearing completion, I was offered another business as a partnership to open a restaurant in an enterprise centre and, against my better judgment and the lack of the full information about this big project that I was taking on, I left the canteen and entered a partnership and opened up a restaurant for a year, which went belly up. The stress, worry and fear were so much that It kept me awake at night. My partner walked away as he had other commitments and I was left with the lot. This took me down into the deepest darkest black hole from which I thought there was no return, my light and passion for life went out. My journey from then on was very dark, I simply fell apart. I couldn't cope with feeling that I was a failure and I continued to beat myself up. I couldn't sleep, I was in so much distress, I couldn't talk to anyone about how I was feeling until a friend suggested I ask for help. I turned to my family who took me to the doctor.

The doctor prescribed a cocktail of medication, which left me even more suppressed and sedated. It was a long road being in the dark, I wasn't sure of anything anymore. I was scared and confused. Sometimes I thought my life had ended. My family at that time were also scared as they didn't know what to do to help me, it was never discussed, it was like an unspoken fear between us. Looking back, it must have been very tough for them seeing me like this. The road to recovery seemed endless, and over those three years of ups and the downs I felt more isolated. One of the biggest challenges for me was that I didn't feel in control of my own life.

I remember sitting at the dinner table one day looking at my two beautiful boys with fear and anxiety in their eyes. They were then aged five and nine. I knew I needed to speak with them and wasn't quite sure what to say. I somehow got the words out and asked them how they were doing. They both started to cry, as did I. At that moment a strength and power came from within me and I reassured them that I wasn't going to die, I was sick, and I just needed some time to heal and get better. We hugged each other and suddenly I realised that strength and power within was like a spark of light inside, a spark I had known so well, and it turned on again. I recognised it as the same feeling I had at different times in my life. I knew I was safe and with that I was able to start my journey back to health.

Each day I dug deep down inside myself to connect with that inner strength. I knew I could never go back to life in the fast lane, rushing around. It was like I had a rebirth as nothing was the same anymore for me. Day by day, one step at a time, I started to rebuild my life and my health. I attended medical practitioners, counsellors and nutritionists and I found some healers that I worked with. This started to bring balance back into my life and I came off all the medication. I noticed that the spark was getting stronger.

I remember taking the two boys out for a walk one day and the sun was shining. I was happy to be alive again. One of my sons had brought his scooter with him and when he got tired, he said, 'Mam why don't you have a go? You will enjoy it.' and I did. Now I must say, I got a few funny looks from people driving by in their cars, as the boys ran along beside me, while I scooted along and had a good laugh. This was the first time in such a long time that I felt my joy return and it was great to see the boys happy again.

I continued my journey of discovery and became interested in holistic therapies, where I learned about looking at the whole person, physically mentally, emotional and spiritually, as one unit. I now know that if one of these parts are out of balance, we don't work so well.

I started to learn about my body and how to get the best from it. Nutrition was one key factor and exercise was another.

Regarding my mental health, I realised that, through all the years that I worked under the huge pressure of trying to achieve work-life balance, and had the drive to study and succeed, it took a toll on me, leaving me mentally drained.

Spiritually, this was easy for me to practice, as all through my life the things that made me happy, such as singing, dancing, being around like-minded happy people, having a good laugh, and spending time with people who inspired and supported me, allowed my spirit out to play and it was beautiful. I learned to keep a gratitude journal and write down each morning and evening five or more things I was grateful for. Another useful tool for me was writing some of my happy memories to remind myself of those good times, which brought a feel-good factor that raised my energy level, especially on days when my energy was not so good.

Emotionally, I needed to learn to let go rather than holding on to the unwanted hurts or criticism that I had experienced, and I continued to remind myself daily to do so. The more I learned about me as a whole person, the more balanced I became, and the more aware I became of this energy that was inside me, the energy that even grows our hair and digests our food. Have you ever thought about how our internal organs work, without us having to do anything? We don't even have to tell ourselves to breathe. It's fascinating when you start to learn how it works, and you start to understand this same energy controls everything from the planets to Mother Nature and the animals. It is the very same energy that is inside us and I also believe that's why a lot of people love spending time in nature, it's a feel-good factor connecting energy to energy. I became so fascinated with this that I decided to attend a twelve-day seminar to learn more about life source energy. It was like the missing piece of the puzzle that I had been looking for most of my life, wanting to know who I am and what is this life all about. Taking this trip took courage and strength and it cost a lot of money. I knew it meant leaving my family behind, but sometimes, you have to take that leap of faith and follow your inner guidance, even if it's at a cost of money, friendships or family. At that stage it was a matter of saving my own life and sanity. I knew somehow it was something I needed to do for me.

On the first day of the seminar I felt the presence of the teacher when he entered the room, although I had never met him before, I somehow felt I knew him. I sensed an energy coming from him. That might seem a strange thing to say but it wasn't strange at all. I don't have the space to explain it all in this chapter, but I am sure you know what I mean. Have you ever met somebody for the first time and you feel as if, you have known them all your life? It's like that old familiar feeling. It feels like home, like coming home to yourself. It seemed like the most natural feeling in the world and I knew this feeling so well.

As the days progressed, one of the things I learned was the real meaning of the word education, this was something that got my attention and I became even more curious to know about myself from the inside. We were never told that growing up, we were giving all this education to learn to become somebody or something better but never told we were good enough, that's the way it was then. That is the part of me I loved to express as a child and as a young mother, and all the drive I had to create everything in my life, was in fact inside me and it is called my spirit. Throughout the twelve days we were given all this new information and the tools to re-educate ourselves from the inside out. When we learned how to really relax and completely let go, this power that is within all of us became more readily available. These exercises unleashed the power within my whole body and mind and the experience was profound. For the first time, I felt I was plugged into life. I suppose one needs to have experienced this for themselves to truly understand the value of knowing the truth that lies within everyone.

I also learned that no matter what you have achieved or accomplished in your life up to now, it is only a small fraction of the bigger picture. The only way to re- educate yourself and explore the real part of yourself is to learn how your mind and spirit really work, from the inside out. This part of us knows more about us than we do. The reason that we feel separate from it, is because of our divided mind and the thoughts we think, such as 'I would love a holiday' followed by the thought 'but I can't afford it.' You stop yourself before you even look at the possibilities of how it could be possible. In my experience, I have now learned to decide on what It is I want; like a holiday and decide I am having it. I step into my power and feel this rush of energy that flows out through every cell of my body. It's like my turbo power is switched on, I know what I want, and I know I am having it, so I let it go without a second thought, in the certainty that the perfect way to receiving or achieving this is always shown. Now I must say this requires me to have 100% faith and trust in the power that lies within, this is where trust comes in to play. My experience of this beautiful spirit is that it's a perfect loving intelligence and only wants the best for us all.

After coming back from the seminar, it took a long time for me to realise my real journey was only beginning as I started to uncover the truth of who I really am, which is a free spirit that needs to be expressed out into the world, as we all have our own unique expression. If this is left lying dormant and hidden through fear, we can get sick and feel suppressed or depressed. I now know that when I wasn't using my gifts, talents and creative abilities, it was then I felt cut off from life. After the seminar, I started channelling my energy into training as a holistic therapist. I worked in a health store for seven years, learning about food supplements and nutrition, and I became a massage therapist and a Reiki Master healer, train the trainer certified, so I could put together workshops, weekend retreats and seminars. I recently received my certificate for becoming a life coach. All this is my new-found passion and I love to share all this information to help people to become aware of who they are and help them uncover their true self.

I need to remind myself daily of the importance of keeping balance in all areas of my life, so I practice relaxation every day and I go for walks in nature. As I walk along, being present I become more aware of the sensitivity and pureness of my spirit, as it flows through me. This beautiful connection between us grows every time I connect to it and so it becomes a new way of living, happiness, peace and unconditional love, all coming from inside me. I suppose it's just like meeting someone you fancy for the first time, a girlfriend or boyfriend that you would like to spend time with and get to know. This spirit is the very same, we need to take the time to go inside and connect with ourselves and grow the relationship. It's the best feeling ever, you just know you are so loved and cherished. I love to spend time connecting inside myself, sitting quietly and being in the present moment, without thoughts. It allows my energy to move through me freely and it can heal my body, leaving me feeling relaxed and peaceful. I attend a class every week with like-minded energetic people to continue to learn and grow my spirit. The connection gets better and stronger and this has become a big part of my life. I know it keeps me safe and I don't look outside myself anymore for answers. I have included a few tips from my daily routine, below, to help you do the same, if it's something you would like for yourself.

The Daily Routine

- Tune in - First thing in the morning I connect to my spirit
- Gratitude - I give thanks for all the things I have in my life right now,
- Intention - I set an intention of good things for myself, my family and the world, for the day ahead.
- Body cleanse – I drink a cup of boiled water with a slice of lemon to cleanse before I eat, and I have a piece of fruit.

- Meditate - After breakfast I love to sit quietly and meditate for fifteen minutes
- Connect to Nature - I like to go for a walk as this is where I have learned to be present
- Happy memories - I take the time to ponder over some of my happy memories and I write them down. I often bring myself back to a happy event. Most times I find it gives me even more good memories. It's like opening my happy memories Album, which is stored in my mind. This is the foundation for feeling good. When you continue to do this regularly, these memories store in the front of your mind and on any days when you're not feeling so good, you can recall them easily to change your state, so you feel a lot better.
- State Changers - I need to remind myself daily of the importance of keeping balance in my life, so I practice relaxation and walking in nature. Sometimes if I'm not in a good place, I put on my music and dance, dance, dance. This is a great way of letting go, I allow the music to bring me into the present moment. It clears my head, and this is one way of changing state. Calling a friend, arranging to meet or watching a feel-good movie are also some of the things I do to instantly change my mental state to bring up those good vibes

- Diet - Most days I try to eat a healthy balanced diet. Fresh vegetables, fish or turkey, sweet potatoes, salads and small amounts of brown bread. I do binge sometimes but mostly stick to health food. I find certain supplements are needed in my diet and I try to drink only filtered distilled water.
- Sleep - I love my sleep and it's essential to a good mental state. I try to get eight hours most nights.

Thank you for taking the time to read my chapter. I am so grateful that I had the opportunity to share a small part of my story and hope that it empowers you to unleash your silent hero.

Love and light

Marie.

Acknowledgements

It was a pleasure meeting and collaborating with Donna and all the co-authors of WE Summit Together. Thank you also to my support team: My family, Sophie, Lorraine, Mary and Anne.

Purpose
by Liz Dillon-Valloor

Energy levels were low, my confidence bruised as the initial high of getting my leaving Certificate exam results dissipated. Before the exam, I had a purpose that kept me motivated. I could get out of the family home. There was no future there. However, I soon realised that I needn't expect help or a modicum of advice about my future from my parents. Mentoring was not on my radar or theirs.

The girls in the family were meant to find their own way in life. It was the 1960's. Any request for direction was met with silence. Times were beginning to change and opportunities for women were in their infancy. Though I was one of the top achievers in school, I hadn't a clue what to do. That conversation on what I should do and where I should go never happened. It was clear the boys would run the farm and that was as far as it went.

In a way that focus to get out into the world, took the pre-examination pressure off. The problem with the educational system then was that the pupil was expected to know who or what they wanted to be. However, the choices available to me then were limited. We could join the Convent and be a nun (some were asked to join), we could become Primary School teachers, join the civil service, become nurses or work in a bank, if you were lucky. What was not clear to me then was that none of that had anything to do with who I was as a unique human being. That thought was a luxury.

I had the idea that if I succeeded in the exams, something magically would be offered to me. I did have the notion that I would like to travel the world, to be an air hostess. I was gutted when I learned that it was not possible because I needed glasses. Air hostesses looked like supermodels in those years. What was I to do?

Immediately after the Leaving Certificate exams I was like a rabbit in headlights. A ship without a compass. The previous year I was hyped up on *Beatle* mania. Anything seemed possible in that new and changing world. I could do what I liked in my imagination, so long as it didn't involve money or family investment. It seemed easy when I was on a high, but on a downward spiral I had to confront a new reality and I was scared. The previous summer I worked for John and Pat in Dublin. They were a young couple who needed help looking after their children during the summer months. We worked well together, and they suggested I stay with them until I found a course suitable for me. What I didn't know or understand was that I was burnt out. That was when the panic attacks started. I had no understanding of what was happening to me. One minute I was a bit anxious and the next this engulfing feeling, as if I was having a heart attack. I could tell no one. I thought I was dying. I lay there and prayed it would go away. Somehow, I managed to get up and pretend that all was well.

John and Pat advised that I do a secretarial course in Dunlaoghaire, Co. Dublin. That is what girls like me did. I was willing to try anything. I was doing quite well until one night I got an unmerciful pain in my stomach and was brought down to the hospital. They admitted me thinking it might be an appendix. After many tests the consultant told me that the pains were imaginary, and I was sent home.

I went to my local doctor, a man who had known me since birth and told him my tale of woe, on how I was so lonely in Dublin and found the course stressful. I asked him not to tell my parents, but he must have. He gave me valium and kindly informed me that I needed to pull myself together. I didn't know which was worse the panic attack or the fear of another panic attack.

My parents decided that I should not return to secretarial college but had no other ideas as to what I should do. My mother was crystal clear when she casually announced that I should go out and get a job, any job, as there was nothing for me at home. "You may go to Dublin, I have enough on my plate here, without having to deal with you". That casual statement was made as she was making an apple tart. My heart sank even lower, if that was possible. My father brought me to Pat and John's house, handed me ten shillings and declared, "All the best". I was a to start my life on that. It was my only option. I was happy to help them mind the children in this transitional phase.

I didn't want to be a burden to Pat and John either so the next day I took a bus into town and went into a recruitment agency. I had to get something because if I didn't, I couldn't stay with this family forever. I must have looked like a sad creature as I walked into the office of *Alfred Bird & Sons*. They offered me a job in the Order Department. They had a factory in Ship St and made jelly and *Birds Custard*. In fairness to the staff and management, they were extremely kind and trained me well. They sent me on a course to learn how to type.

A year later all Irish banks were on strike. To deal with the backlog after the strike they recruited new staff. I knew my parents were ashamed that I worked in a jelly factory, so I hoped to please them by applying for a position in the bank. I didn't let anyone know of my intention, in case I wasn't successful. I had a dreadful need to be accepted, to be loved. I was delighted to hear I got in. My sense of purpose was back and in full swing as I read the acceptance letter. I had a week's training and visualized myself in my own apartment in Dublin, free and ready to take on the world.

Immediately I was transferred to a small town in Cavan. There was no accommodation for women. The male staff in the banks had to stay in the local hotel and the women in what was known as digs. A bedroom and meals provided. I could hear the mice running around in the attic at night. It certainly wasn't as I had imagined bank life to be like.

I met my future husband who happened to work in another bank. It was 1972. Women had to *resign* on marriage. At twenty years old I had to write that letter of resignation. Here I was again in a cul-de-sac. What was I to do? Now with wisdom garnered from my experience the most important question is not what you want to do, because that answer is based on the experiences you are familiar with, but W*ho do you want to be? Who inspires you?* I had no female role models that resonated with me. It was normal then to get married very young. I was not aware of it at the time, but I had downloaded a very important mental programme – *Do not upset other people. Do not express your feelings because other people will suffer. Whatever you do you please the father and mother architypes in your life. You do not upset the siblings* *in your family either and you do everything you can to help others at your expense.* I brought this programme with me into my marriage and every office I worked in. Any time I went to voice my feelings I ended up apologizing for upsetting the other. I had absolutely no voice before an authority figure. I spent my time figuring out what they wanted to hear, and I regurgitated it back to them.

The only thing I knew was that I hated being dependent. Trapped with no freedom, no purpose. I had witnessed my mother having to ask my father for every shilling. It was very humiliating trying to justify every item while he had the freedom to do what he liked. My new purpose was linked to financial freedom. I had to find a way. It had nothing to do with finding work that suited me or my abilities. I had no awareness or value on them. I would have scrubbed floors sooner than go cap in hand for money. Financial freedom became my new mantra. Thankfully, three months after I married, women were allowed return to work on a temporary basis in public service employment. Within a year, I was made permanent. Ireland had joined the European Economic Community.

Life Happens, my response to the happenings, the daily challenges were the problem. Downloaded mind Apps in unawareness are like a cancer undetected. I was like a robot reacting to the beliefs I had garnered over the years. It was difficult to stay on track with a vision for my life when my beliefs about who I was were dictating how I should be to please other people. My brain was like a metal detector on the lookout for disapproval signs.

My newly acquired mother-in-law wasn't happy with my working in the bank. It wasn't a suitable job if we were to have a family. She wanted me to do Primary teaching. My family would have turned up their noses at Primary teachers and I knew it. Whenever there was a mention of Primary teachers the image of Aran cardigans, cold dusty classrooms and barefooted children was the subject of conversation. There was no family history of teaching. Both her parents were Principals in Primary schools. I felt I was being pushed towards something that had nothing to do with me and everything to do with her.

It happened that University College Dublin were on strike. While I was working in the Bank of Ireland Montrose branch, I had lunch with my younger sister who was in her first year of University. This made the University less threatening as I met with other students. I began to feel the possibility that I could manage this. I had an underlying feeling that if I got a degree, it would be the missing piece in my own emotional development. Once I had that piece of paper, perhaps I would be able to speak out on what was important for me.

There was no internet, Google or an Open Day to help me choose my next step, just a small voice within me that whispered tentatively do this. I took a deep breath, moved through a wall of fear, went up to Administration and signed up to do a Bachelor of Arts degree specializing in Geography, History and Economics. I knew mother-in-law would be very angry, and I wasn't disappointed. It was easier to ask for forgiveness than permission. The deed was done.

My childhood experience developed my ability to over-control my feelings and emotions. I had no voice. If I explained my feelings, I was told I was only upsetting the household. To ask for financial help would deprive others. If you gave an opinion, it was guaranteed to be ridiculed. When you achieved success, you were asked to tone your enthusiasm. "Who do you think you are? Rising above your station, a cut above buttermilk, are we?" I had no understanding that I was in this category. I saw my nice person image as being normal, even if I knew what I wanted I was afraid to ask. The feelings of guilt were too much. Though it may have been wise to hold back at home, I continued the pattern, even in situations where it was safe to speak. I needed to feel safe and to do this I suppressed feelings. My registering for a course that I wanted to do was like climbing Everest.

Over-controlled children and adults control themselves, under-controlled control everyone around them. They feel very entitled and can create a storm until someone gives in to their demands. Neither personality is happy. Understanding your role in relationships is the first step to freedom. At that time, I did not see how damaging my programme was and how it impacted every area of my life. I just knew that I could not discuss the course I was choosing with my mother-in-law because she was a force to be reckoned with.

I had savings so knew I was financially able to do this. My biggest fear wasn't money, it was my fear that I wasn't intelligent enough. To move forward you must face your fears. It was a true case of feel the fear and do it anyway.

The lectures were amazing. I came alive listening to new ways of thinking. However, I had no study skills. We learned by rote in school and were told what to learn. I now had to choose, to form independent thinking and to pass exams. I did not understand that I was an experiential learner and how to approach my study in a way that suited me. I needed to have some reference point as to where I could apply my learning to life, to make connections. I seemed to have a million facts to digest but facts were not applicable to my life. That was when I felt overwhelmed. Somehow, I crammed knowledge into me to allow me pass exams. Of what use was that? Three year's hard study and the joy of learning how to learn, learning to improve my skills was crushed by not understanding how I learned. I could never fully achieve my potential until I understood that. Some people need to hear information, some see, and others experience. This is not considered in our educational system and many children either suffer unnecessary stress or drop out. People say to me, "My child is not an academic". I don't agree with this. Your child could be an amazing academic but he or she is not being taught in a way that is suitable for them.

In my final year, I was expecting our first baby. I had to really make myself focus through the exhaustion and sickness. I didn't want to repeat exams as they were too close to her due date. That reality certainly creates purpose for you. I couldn't get a placement in a school to allow me study for a Higher Diploma in Education because of my need for maternity leave.

My daughter was a few weeks old when my mother-in- law discovered a course that would allow me to become a Primary Teacher. Now that my daughter was born, I could see the sense of it, but I just wanted a bit of time to recover and enjoy being with her.

Mother- in-law was a woman on a mission. She was determined I do this. She saw the importance of my having an independent income, if something happened to her son.

She had been through that experience when her husband contacted Tuberculosis. I understood her motivation, but did I really want teaching? The energy she brought to this vision was remarkable. It was a polarity. My parents had no interest and she was its polar- opposite. My learning was to bring me forward out of the stagnation of my childhood and develop insight and courage to communicate my feelings to my mother-in-law to find my own balance. Hindsight is wonderful.

I completed the course and got a temporary teaching position. I loved the course, particularly the psychological aspect of teaching. Understanding how children learn fascinated me. How to apply my new-found knowledge to thirty children with different ability and interest levels was mind boggling. Children and adults must have a purpose for learning and to help them find it you need to understand what is of importance to them in their lives. It must interest them and to do that they must be involved. I enjoyed being with the children but was like a square peg in a round hole in the system. I had no room to explore ideas and felt suffocated. Even as a small child I was asked to mind my younger siblings and I seemed to have a way to calm them. I loved being around children because of their honest way of communicating. What I needed to accept was the reality that I had a talent with children. That creating an environment that catered for the well- being of children was one of my highest values. I had never ever looked at my life in that way.

I was expecting our second daughter and internally I decided not to return to teaching. We were also moving to a new house. The house was under construction and I asked if we could convert the garage into a room. I had a plan mulling in my head to run my own pre-school. I never said a word for fear of being stopped. My husband and mother-in-law were singing from the same hymn sheet and I didn't think I had the ability to withstand the pressure.

I bided my time until we were settled in our new home. By that time, I had an image in my mind. I wanted to be independent and learn from the children how they learned. I also wanted it to be for four days a week, to allow me- time with my own children.

It was in that little pre-school that I saw how an inability to express feelings was damaging. I witnessed my mirror. I observed children at play and how some gave in easily to the demands of more dominant children, how they put themselves last. I created a safe space to help them voice their needs and wants. The more dominant children also needed my attention. Their skills in communication were also poor. They feared not getting their needs met and any attention was better than none. We worked on that and almost always by the end of the year we had a harmonious group. What helped was the input from parents. Once they understood what I was doing they were onboard. I taught the children a skill I had to learn for myself around adults. Children are more receptive to changing behaviors. I could be my ideal self with the children but not with dominant adults.

One little girl loved being in the group so much she refused to change to a five-day pre-school the following year. She came to me because she had problems relating to her own age group. Those issues got solved very quickly and we had a wonderful time.

Her brother was easier to handle, so her Mum said she couldn't take the risk of sending him to me as he too might refuse to leave.

Your feelings are the language of your soul. My purpose, though I didn't realise it at the time, was to be a mentor for children. I had a much greater interest in their wellbeing than cramming knowledge into them. Once I connected with a child, gained their trust, found out exactly where they were on the learning ladder, I could lead them to become confident learners. Seeing their joy at achieving absolutely inspired me. I knew I had made the right decision. I did not have the confidence before to stick to my beliefs about learning because I had no personal experience of it working. With fourteen years of how wellbeing comes first, a purpose must be part of their learning, building on a child's understanding step by step I was on track to create confident children. Talent is important and the opportunity to develop that talent, coupled with personality and purpose. If one of these is missing, then it will not work out. Children are no different to us adults. They too need a sense of purpose. They must be able to apply what they are learning to what is of value to them in their lives. They love from an early age to be part of the household, to have responsibility because it gives them a feeling of self- worth. In our busy lives we can exclude them and because we are so busy, we can't take the time for them to complete tasks.

In the meantime, my own personal life was being challenged. Through reading every self-help book available and attending workshops I began my own inner transformation.

When I read Anthony de Mello's book *Awareness*, I fully comprehended my role in creating my unhappiness. If I was reacting, if I was voiceless, then I had downloaded an app in my childhood that prevented me from being able to comfortably express myself. Another person, in another environment, would have a different set of beliefs about themselves. He said I would get in touch with my unique set of beliefs through my reactions to people and situations. I could identify my beliefs, check them out and change them if I chose.

I began to observe me. I saw how I was massively controlled by my mother-in-law. It seemed too much of a task. I came up with all types of excuses as to why I shouldn't stand up to her. I began small. I experimented with saying no to people not in my immediate circle. You would think I was coming off drugs. The powerful effect of guilt on the body is extraordinary, the terror of rejection, not being good enough. Until then I did not fully comprehend the extent of my dislike of myself. Unless I had validation from an external source I was depressed. This need had turned me into a human doing, trying to please everybody and nobody. Every job I had I worked myself to the bone to please the Manager. The only validation I could accept was when I was praised. I never looked at me and said that work you did was excellent, how you solved that problem was insightful. Unless I got that validation, I belittled me. That need was intense, which made me intense. I couldn't enjoy life or take time out. I could not even buy myself a perfume. I could only buy something for me if I bought something for each member of my family. Good clothes were bought to look well at Sunday Mass. I was slowly turning into mother-in-law. I needed to do and be all that was important for her. I was suffering from good-child syndrome as an adult.

Looking at how disempowered I was, I believed my biggest challenge was mother-in-law. To help tackle this I went to my father-in-law's grave in Glasnevin cemetery. I loved him. He was a powerful male role model. Though I only knew him for three years, his loving presence is always with me. I spilled out my tales of woe to him, not really expecting my prayers to be answered. From that day on I never felt obliged to do something for her that came as a demand, nor did I stay silent if she criticized one of my children, or me. Her criticisms were always prefaced with "If you don't mind my saying". After that announcement came a stinging comment, to which I then had the courage to say "Actually I do mind. I do not think you have a right to criticize". Initially, she demanded her heart pills but got over it. I was respectful but not an iota of guilt. I had had enough.

When you have hidden your innermost feelings away in a sealed container for over forty years it can be unsettling as you try to discover your true self minus the beliefs and habits of a lifetime. I found walking on a beach, or in a park with my dog very soothing. When I needed to express how I wished to experience change in line with how I truly felt I went for a walk to rehearse what I wanted to say. Up until that time I was easily manipulated back into my supplicant self, now having seen truth I could communicate clearly. I became a broken record. No matter what guilt trip was shoveled on top of me I remained calm and stated, "It's the way I feel". I understood reading Awareness that I did not have the power to change another human being. Change began with me. I soon experienced the freedom of giving an opinion, choosing to do something important for me and taking time out. To find my values became my new purpose. Once I could identify them, then I knew what route to take. One thing was for sure I would look at every reaction in my body, see what the feeling was saying to me. Times I was so upset I needed to soothe it, until I could see if I needed to do something or perhaps not do something. I was over involved in solving other people's problems. Now, stopping, discerning if I needed to become involved freed me.

I went to Achill Island to breathe. My husband did not want to look at the chasm that was emerging and I continued my journey of self- discovery. The more I emptied out old ideas of who I was, the more my unique self-emerged. I was a totally different person to the one he married. We separated January 1996.

In December 1996 I started my Primary teaching career in Archbishop McQuaid National school. It was a designated disadvantaged school. Here I was challenged to implement all the principles of learning I had found successful. It was more difficult at first, as the children were older. Many had lost interest in learning because of their experiences and I was forced to look within me for solutions on how to respond to challenging behaviours. Every time I met with resistance, I observed my feelings of insecurity. I adapted how I reacted to gain the child's trust. I had to develop a keen eye. They were used to arguing and blaming and if I tried to force them to behave, it never worked. If there was a disagreement among them, I carefully listened to both sides and allowed them to come to a solution. I learned to stay away from that famous word WHY. The moment you ask, "Why did you do that?" "What were you thinking?", the shutters go down. Trust is broken.

One boy punched another in Assembly. Knowing his mother was in the parent's room he ran to her and created a very powerful story. She demanded the other boy apologize. I was told to get an apology out of him. I felt that I would wait to hear more. It takes time to get to the root of a problem, but it is worthwhile as it saves so much more time later as the children learn how to problem solve. I sat them down. They sat there sullen faced. The perpetrator declared he would not apologize. I said that I was not asking him to. What I was looking for was the truth. From my point of view if one boy strikes out at another then there must be some action that instigated it. Knowing this duo, I knew this was probably the case. I explained to the victim that I could make the other apologize but if he had any part in it, it would be impossible for them to be friends for a long time. Apologizing for something that you did but the other had a part in it too can create more trouble down the road. The perpetrator will only be looking for revenge as soon as he can get it. I told them no one was going to get punished, but I did want the truth so that they could properly solve the problem. It was then the victim owned up to calling him names on the way in to the Assembly when no one was listening and the other reacted. They both laughed and that was the end of it.

Over time powerful change happened. I began to respect my talent with children.

I continued to do what I did best. Look after the well-being. Remove fears around learning, find what was of interest to them, link what I needed to teach them to their experiences. I needed to find their strengths, build on them so that they would then feel comfortable with addressing gaps in their learning. I became more passionate about their learning as time went by. Praising the child created the good child syndrome, praising the achievements, the effort was very powerful in building their self-esteem. Each time a child succeeded they filled an internal bucket with courage, skill and satisfaction. Over time their confidence soared. I had to find where they were last comfortable in learning. A young girl could not do mathematics. She had signed off on them. I found where she was on the ladder of learning and began from there. Every week in the test I put a minimum of four challenges on the paper that I knew she could do. Then I added a few to see if she could manage them. Each time I told her the test was for me so that I could see what it is I needed to teach her. Over six weeks she gained confidence and I could move her forward. Her father came to the school and asked what I had done. He had given up on her. I said the first thing I did was to remove her fear. Once I did that, I could teach her anything. What I was doing for them was sharing my wisdom, mentoring them in a way that was not available to me in my childhood. The reward was seeing them shine.

Life is interesting as it steers you down this road and that. When I was prepared to listen to my own inner self, change was possible. Too many images of what I should be, how I should look, how I should behave kept me away from my own higher values. Ignore your inner voice at your peril. Your creativity is blocked by your need of external approval. Who AM I is the most important question? Who do I want to be? Who inspires me?

I had been living my life through the lens of other people. I was allowing my life to be dictated by the familiar.

Working on my own transformation I could release my fears and begin to explore my life.

I didn't have a parenting roadmap. I stumbled through those years. I knew that I could not lead them when my own leadership skills were undeveloped. I could not teach them how to have a voice when I was voiceless. I was training them from my own skillset. I was one of those mums who brought their children to every class to build their self-esteem. The most powerful influence in our children's lives are ourselves. To be able to bring about change I did not have to change them. They were fine. I needed to change me. I needed my children to see me walk the talk. They had to find their voice, stand up for their truth, say no to people, find out what their highest values were, what resonated with them, and live their lives. I needed to show them what responsibility to self looks like. I made many mistakes as a parent but can truthfully say at every stage I was traversing new territory. We are all here to evolve and my children will go beyond my parenting skills. That is how we move forward, that is life.

Before changing my own mind, I could only see them through my old lens. That old lens was filthy with old outdated programmes. I was trying my best to be the best parent through a filter that was harmful for them. I could not see their individual talents or have the courage to stand up for them as they explored new avenues in their lives. I was not comfortable in allowing them shine because it was out of my comfort zone. I was engulfed in the familiar until my eyes were opened to that reality. That was until I saw me sleepwalking through my life and expecting my children, and the children I taught, to sleepwalk through theirs.

This journey took me to Anthony de Mello's Centre, *Sadhana Institute*, Lonavla. India where I facilitated seminars in Awareness, to Norte Dame in Ohio and to the Theosophical Society in Auckland, while at the same time I continued to teach at the school. The children were my light. They mirrored to me any untruth. They made me stand up for them, to show them that it is possible. I developed a school garden for the children who had a difficulty sitting in a classroom all day. Though they were only nine years old, they dug that garden with me. We got funding and plants from various places and it was a huge success. We decided to enter it in a competition. Two adjudicators came out to inspect. I was fully aware that there were other middle-class schools in the same competition with everything from willow tunnels to waterfalls, but I didn't care. We were happy.

The day of reckoning came, and the ladies asked them pertinent questions. It was clear they loved their garden and we got news we had won a prize. We were down in the Town Hall in Dunlaoghaire waiting our turn to go up for our photograph when a more senior teacher told me that only the children in proper uniform could go. I looked down at the faces and saw one anxious face. He sat there with his shaved head, silver ear-ring and tatty jumper. He also had a reputation for disruptive behavior. He looked me straight in the eye. I was only a temporary teacher, with four children needing my salary. The truth in those eyes went straight like an arrow into my heart. When our name was called, I asked all the children to stand up and go for the photo. I knew I was in for a lecturing when I returned. I survived, but I would not have survived internally if I did not be the light those children needed to see that day. Fear had controlled me, then I needed to move through it one day at a time.

I now understand that you must listen to the quickening of your heart, look around your home, feel what makes your heart sing and you will soon discover what is of highest value to you. Observe your reactions to people and to situations and see if you are allowing others dictate the terms of your life. Without all the negative dross accumulated over the years you can now give you permission to sing your song and shine in a way that allows the world to see and experience the light you truly are. That is the ultimate purpose in life.

As the song says, "Sweet mystery of life, at last I've found you". Be you, everyone else is taken.

Living Life to Your Values
by Melanie Ardoin

Have you ever noticed how much pressure there is in our culture telling us to do more, be more, and achieve more? Our lives are burdened by an over-filled, cluttered, full schedule, we are always 'busy', and expecting so much of ourselves. There are too many responsibilities and not enough time in the day or energy to accomplish everything you want to do. We are living in a time where, despite their busy-ness, people are feeling a lack of meaningfulness in their lives, record levels of depression, stress and fatigue. *(reference Arianna Huffington 'Thrive').*

As a Separation and Divorce Coach, Simple Single Parenting Blogger, and single mom of two young children myself, I often work with people trying to balance so many things on their plates while dealing with a large amount of stress and change in their lives. My main aim is to support and assist people through these changes by providing an empathetic space, while also helping them to declutter their lives to allow for fresh, positive changes to take place.

I've been fortunate to have a very good life for the most part, and to have a wonderful, supportive family. Despite all my fun adventures, my life has had its dark moments as well. I've been badly bullied, drugged and raped, mentally and physically abused, lived in a shelter with my children, separated from my husband, made redundant from work and on the edge of financial ruin and bankruptcy. Not something you would expect from someone brought up in an upper-middle class environment, yet not something unique either from what I'm learning. This is not the right space to delve further into those stories- what I want you to know is it is such a feeling of freedom, such a weight off your shoulders, when you can learn not to hate anymore, to forgive, to move on from your 'stories' and realise whatever has happened in the past is past, you own your life story and you can change the direction any time you REALLY want to- the only one you are hurting by holding on to resentment is yourself. I have forgiven, moved on, looked at my values and thought- what do I want to make of my one life? I have learnt to forgive myself too, something often missed yet so vital- it's OK not to be perfect. 'Onwards and upwards' has always been my motto- I could choose to focus on those negative times in my life, or to turn the page, start again, and use the awareness of what I learnt from these episodes to live an even fuller life now and help others in the process - the end goal is to create a vision of a new life more full of meaning and fulfilment, and to love your life (and yourself). As the great philosopher Alfred Adler taught, "No matter what has occurred in your life up to this point, it should have no bearing on how you choose to live your life from now on… people can change and be happy from this moment forward, the problem is not one of ability but one of courage."

What I seek to help my clients understand is that a meaningful and fulfilled life doesn't necessarily come from achieving the next promotion, the bigger house, the fancier car or the approval of friends and family - that life needs to be lived from more than just FOMO (Fear of Missing out). That we all need to embrace the opportunity to recreate our lives based on continuously reviewed values and our daily contribution to others. In the words of Brenee Brown, I assist my clients in living their lives more 'wholeheartedly'.

Values are key. They unlock the opportunity to experience a gentle, internal peace and happiness, different to the ever-fleeting happiness we try to get from the usual societal trophies we always chase.

"We have searched for happiness in a bigger pay check...only to discover we immediately desired an even bigger one.

We have searched for happiness in a job promotion or recognition...only to discover the accolades don't last.

We have searched for happiness in bigger homes...only to discover they are accompanied by burdensome mortgage payments.

We have searched for happiness in fancier cars...only to discover they get scratches and dings just like the others.

We have searched for happiness in alcohol and drugs and sex...only to discover the pleasure has disappeared by morning.

We have searched for happiness in large savings accounts...only to discover money can't solve all our problems.

When a pursuit does not provide lasting fulfilment, we have two choices. First, we can chase after it harder and harder,

hoping it will eventually satisfy. Or second, we can reject that pursuit altogether. Choose the latter."

- Joshua Becker

I moved away from an unhealthy marriage quite suddenly three years ago, my son was only one year old at the time and my daughter was only three. As with most single parents, it's not usually something anyone plans or wants and it took time to make the decision, not to mention the adjustment after, but it was something I had to do in order to respect myself. It also gave me an opportunity to transform, to see what other areas could be changed to help me move towards the life I wanted, a life that is lived according to my own values. It hasn't always been easy - it has taken a lot of work and perseverance and plenty of trust in life, and is a work in progress, but along the way I've be able to share my experiences by helping others in similar situations. It's been a tumultuous and emotional three years but through our own separate growth, a lot of diplomacy, and love for our children, my ex-husband and I are now on friendly terms again. This Christmas eve we all met up for pizza and to watch the *Mary Poppins Returns* movie together with the kids and spend time together for the kids' birthdays also. In the end, our shared value of being able to jointly parent our two children and provide as solid a grounding for them as possible despite our separation has made it much easier to move forward on positive terms than continue holding grudges.

What are my Values and how can I find them?

Personal values are the general expression of what is most important to you. Values are formed in early childhood, and as we mature, we should take the time to more consciously re-evaluate these and make changes. Your values form your character. They can change when a big event happens in your life or something that causes you to consciously re-evaluate your life. They are also critical to your well-being, as one of the most fulfilling things you can do is live life in harmony with your personal values- they help us decide how to spend our time, energy, and money in a way that's meaningful to us, and lead us to contribute towards others which leads to true happiness.

"Your time is limited, so don't waste it living someone else's life. Don't be trapped by dogma — which is living with the results of other people's thinking. Don't let the noise of others' opinions drown out your own inner voice. And most important, have the courage to follow your heart and intuition. They somehow already know what you truly want to become. Everything else is secondary."

- *Steve Jobs*

I first learnt about the concept of 'Values' when I was undertaking my Diploma in Life, Business and Executive Coaching over nine years ago, while pregnant with my daughter. The activity we undertook then, which you can find in many Values exercises online or in books, was to choose ten words that really resonated with us from a page of words we were given. You then ordered them by importance, by comparing two values and asking, 'Which one is most important to me, if I could only choose one of these?' Put the winner of this on top of a new list and continue down your list. You do this for all 10 words until you have an ordered list of your top 10 values. That, we were told, was how you could discover what your values were and what your top three were following further discussion with your classmates.

This seems to be a common exercise I see in various books and is a good start. However, in my experience discovering your values takes a lot more time, internal exploration and "peeling back the onion" as they say. You see, we often choose our values from a list like this based on what society and other strong personalities in our lives would like us to choose, the "right" thing to do, going along like sheep with what everyone expects of us, rather than what we really feel deep down inside, the uniqueness that is you, and it's so engrained in us it's very difficult to look past it as it's unconscious. In order to really peel back the onion, deeper work and other exercises really need to be done also.

An exercise I often use is to write your own eulogy (and by the way I can honestly say I feel like I've lived my life to the fullest and am completely grateful for everything it has brought me). Arianna Huffington wrote about eulogies in her book *Thrive*, "A eulogy is about how people remember us and how we live in the minds and hearts of others… what we gave, how we connected, how much we meant to our family and friends, small kindnesses, lifelong passions, and the things that made us laugh." David Brooks writes that eulogies "describe the person's care, wisdom, truthfulness and courage. They describe the million little moral judgements that emanate from that inner region" from your values. It is useful to then compare this back to the life you were currently living and look at what tweaks, small or large, you might want to make with your one life, and check in on your direction towards this from time to time. It's easy to get swayed off-course by other people's visions. If you don't control your own life there are plenty of people out there who will happily control it for you.

Another exercise I found particularly helpful was writing out a week or even a month in your ideal life. Make up a story of your ideal life, what you do each day, Monday to Sunday. How do you feel? What do you smell? What do you sense? Who is with you? - almost like a dream. Set your mind free, be as ridiculous as you like. Write down every word that comes to your mind, don't try to stop the flow. You might like to write it for the present, more realistically initially, and then write it for what you would do if you retired, won the lotto or didn't have to work. Compare the two. What are the trends, what do you see repeating? What are you doing, who are you with, what are your surroundings? Highlight a few key words that describe those ideal lives or trends. Analyse them further, can you go a level deeper and find a better word that brings a few of them together under one heading, or a few headings? Compare this back to your initial Top 10 list of words, is there any similarity between those words and what you had on your initial list, is there anything that jumps out at you? This will help you to look at the gap between the life you are living and the life you actually want to live.

Another exercise I often give my clients is to imagine their life 5 years from now, once all the tumultuous changes they are going through have settle down- this often helps them to see past the immediate hurdles and issues, and to envision their lives once these are finally removed, which is often a very positive one. Having that "light at the end of the tunnel" vision is very calming for them and gives them the energy to continue working through the immediate tasks towards their vision. These exercises are just a start to help you on the vital exploration of your values and new life choices. My family moved to a new country every few years as I was growing up. At first, I struggled with all this change, but I eventually learnt to embrace it and see the positive side. In the end, it was a wonderful experience of freedom and adventure, and those were the core values that formed my early 20's which were filled with travel and adventure too. However, as I searched deeper, I realised that Belonging was another very important value for me. I realised that the constant changes had meant that I'd also felt like an outsider, moving from one country to another, always the 'new girl' who had to learn to fit in.

My value of Belonging was the key reason I decided to stop travelling in my mid-twenties, move back to Ireland, return to my roots from where I grew up as a child, and to finally 'grow up' and be more mature. However, I no longer fit in with Ireland either, I wasn't really 'Irish' anymore as I had left Ireland eighteen years beforehand when I was only age seven. Also, coming from six years in the dot-com start-up boom in San Francisco where I straddled both the hippy/rave world, and worked eighty-hours a week at an IT start-up while also completing my MBA; to Dublin where I was expected to settled down, get married, have kids quickly as I was getting "old"; where there weren't even any café's at the time, no vegetarian food, and I was expected to hang out and drink at bars when I didn't even really drink alcohol was a big culture shock. For the past 18 years since I moved "home" in 2001, I have struggled with wanting to belong back in the country I believed I was from- my American accent is still very strong, and even now I grapple to understand the idiosyncrasies and underlying complexities of Irish culture - I still do not "belong" here either. However, as I start to get more involved in my new community we just moved into, a community now richer with people from various cultures and backgrounds I have travelled to in the past, and am brave enough to accept myself, my own values and give those back to the community around me, I feel a sense of fulfilment and belonging to myself and I'm feeling more at peace with being 'different' and just being me.

Dublin is now a thriving, modern melting pot for many foreigners who come here to work and learn English and then try to go home to readjust to their own countries. They too struggle to fit in to their own culture after being away in Ireland for a few years, as their new beliefs and values can change and differ from the community they once came from. So as the world gets smaller and more young people travel, it becomes even more important to "peel back the onion" and fully understand your own values to withstand the culture shock you might experience when you return home.

How can I live my Life to my Values?

White Space- Declutter

Start by de-cluttering your life. Remove inessential pursuits so you can live focused on the things that matter most. Make space to breath, relax, think, let your mind flow. Make space for the truly important things in your life - your values. Give your time and energy to the things that truly matter to you, not the things you feel you should do out of obligation or expectation- do not live to satisfy the expectations of others, have the courage to follow your own life values peacefully, each day at a time.

"I once asked a very successful woman to share her secret with me. She smiled and said to me:

"I started succeeding when I started leaving small fights for small fighters. I stopped fighting those who gossiped about me.

I stopped fighting with my in-laws. I stopped fighting for attention. I stopped fighting to meet people's expectation of me. I stopped fighting for my rights with inconsiderate people. I stopped fighting to please everyone.

I stopped fighting to prove they were wrong about me.
I left such fights for those who have nothing else to fight.
And I started fighting for my vision, my dreams, my ideas

and my destiny. The day I gave up on small fights is the day I started becoming successful and so much more content."
Some fights are not worth your time. Choose what you fight for wisely."

- Dana Ives

Start with a decision on how to spend your time- be adamant about saying 'no' to things that do not align with your values. I found this easiest by writing out a 'stop doing' list. I wrote a list of all the activities in my weekly and monthly schedule and thought for each 'Is the time and energy I am spending on that moving me closer to the things that really matter to me?'.

A simple exercise you can try to help you with this is the 10-10-10 Analysis. It teaches that the way to make decisions is to ask yourself how you will feel about the decision after 10 minutes, 10 months, and 10 years. When you can imagine how you'll feel about any decision in the future, it helps give you the strength and the confidence to make a wise choice in the moment.

I chose one or two things from that list that I was going to stop doing- for example, as a single mom who works full-time I have less 'bonding' time with my kids, I have very little time in my evenings to be with my kids after work before they go to bed, and they spend half the weekend time at their dad's house so we have less time to bond on weekends. I've chosen to stop spending as much time cooking dinners. I throw together simple, healthy meals during the week, and do something more complex on the weekends. Once every two weeks, before the weekends they spend with their dad, we go to a local family restaurant and share a pizza and just have a chill mid-week time together. I also chose to stop allowing my kids to watch TV Monday – Thursday. Instead they spend time in the kitchen with me while I cook, either finishing their homework, or telling me about their day, or even colouring or playing at the kitchen table, as long as we are together in the same room. I keep Sundays for family time as much as possible and try to do something out in nature, I intentionally set aside time for fun and adventure with my kids. Once you've stopped doing a couple of things on your list, move on to the next two, and keep moving through your list until the new habits are more engrained.

I intentionally set aside regular time for rest. I schedule it on my calendar and guard it at all costs. I also block out my family time on my work calendar, from 6:30-9PM to ensure I don't do any work calls then and spend that time with my children- this can be difficult when you're working with global teams across multiple time zones. I try to schedule any evening time-zone calls on one evening per week to keep my other evenings free to catch up on house chores, to rest and call a good friend for a chat- yes I really believe in having an *actual phone conversation* with a close friend or family member, not just texting/messaging/WhatsApp'ing or social media- It makes a world of difference to talk or meet up with people rather than just using social media.

Bucket List

On the opposite spectrum of decluttering is the 'doing'- but not just doing anything. You've probably heard of the 2007 movie 'The Bucket List' starring Jack Nicholson and Morgan Freeman. I've had a bucket list for the last twenty-five years. Every year I plan something fun for myself and tick it off my bucket list. I finished my MBA in International Business which I did part-time while I worked full-time when I was only twenty-two. I helped a start-up go live on the NASDAQ and was a 'paper millionaire' until the Dot com crash (our company almost bought Google at the time...). I've experienced both the fiery passion of a football match in the Buenos Aires stadium, and the inner light of a ten-day intensive Vipassana meditation retreat. I've travelled to all seven continents (including Antarctica), visited over fifty-two countries, and experienced some amazing cultural events such as bathing in the Ganges during the Kumbh Mela in India, helping out at an orphanage in Kenya, and shaking hands with the Dalai Lama and introducing him to my young daughter. I've run the marathon (twice), I've sung with the Dublin Gospel Choir in front of a thousand people at both the Dublin Convention Centre and for a children's charity Laura Lynn at Dublin Croke Park Stadium, and I've recently bought my own little house, a safe haven and home for my two young children and I, and decorated it the way I had always dreamed to. I wrote down each of those bucket list items for a reason because they resonated with my own values at that time and looked at when and how I would achieve each one.

A Life of Meaning

On the other spectrum of doing activities for yourself, is doing activities for others and the wider community. 'The best way to find yourself is to lose yourself in the service of others' – Ghandi. Having my kids participate in some charity events and helping them understand how to appreciate what they have and how they can help others is important to me. Working with support groups such as *WomensAid* or *Alone* (working with elderly who feel alone) speaks to my values also. Have a look back over your own values list and think about how giving back to others might make your life more meaningful, like leaving a sustainable future for your kids and other wider concerns of the community in your values. Remember that happiness and freedom come from following your own values and feeling that these are contributing to others. According to Alfred Adler, one of the founding fathers of Psychology "When one seeks recognition from others and concerns oneself only with how one is judged by others, in the end, one is living other people's lives...and is not living in freedom."

Take That First Step

Declutter your life and your mind- make space for what is truly important to you, your values. Don't worry about making huge changes in your life all at once- you don't need to go out and quit your job, sell your house and move to another country. We move towards making space for our true values by making gradual changes, through our small daily decisions and the habits we choose. Embracing a life of intentional happiness and fulfilment comes in the small moments of life, and sometimes the smallest changes in the way we think or the things we do result in the most powerful results.

Be kind to yourself. Gently push yourself on, be your own cheerleader towards what you know is important to you. Pat yourself on the back for making decisions based on your values, smile to yourself, remember to be your own best friend.

Coming from a freedom-loving, travel and adventure-hungry lifestyle to one of a more subdued Ireland in the early 20's and then settling down into marriage and children was very difficult for me. The constant battle between freedom, family and belonging has raged on in me for many years and I have spent a lot of time understanding and reviewing my values as I have gone through many life changes. I am a work in progress in many areas, and this is one of them. To me, at the moment, having a close relationship with my two young children is of the utmost importance in the few years that remain where they actually want to be with me, before their friends and their own adventures become more important. The decisions I make every single day are based on having quality time with my kids, while mixing in the fun and adventure into our lives together. I am learning to belong to myself and to our little family as a priority and giving back to my little community.

Be a W.I.T.C.H
by Aoife Gaffney

Two of the most powerful words in the English language are "I am".

I am Aoife Gaffney MSc (Hons) BSc (Open) QFA LIB CMC, owner and founder of Prudence Moneypenny Coaching, a money coaching programme designed exclusively for women. I am a wife, parent, entrepreneur, Ireland's first and only Certified Money Coach, Qualified Financial Adviser, certified life coach, NLP master practitioner, bestselling author, tutor, speaker, and mediocre cook. I am not too bad at assembling flat pack furniture. I have lots of other qualifications but there are only so many I can fit on an averaged sized business card. You can find out more about me at www.prudencemoneypenny.com.

I am Irish and I currently live in Kildare, Ireland, with my son, my husband and all their clutter; none of it is mine.

My mission in life is empowering women to achieve financial freedom. Every woman can be a WITCH, – a woman in total control of herself. I work with women to get clarity to discover and achieve their own financial freedom so that they can live their lives on their terms. I help women in a variety of ways including one to one coaching, money mapping, mastermind groups, money circles, writing, speaking engagements and adult education programmes.

Whether you are male or female, you can apply the actions and principles in this chapter to help you enhance your life and start living YOUR life on YOUR terms.

I love my life. I love the freedom it offers me. I love being able to spend time with those that matter to me and I love being able to live my life in accordance with my top three values - freedom, family, and empowerment. Pull up a seat, get comfortable and let me tell you how I have learned so much from my experiences to date and I am finally enjoying the process. I learned to go from financial jail to financial joy and now I am empowering other women to do the same. I have done the hard work, so you don't have to.

My life began nearly fifty years ago at the time of writing. I come from a traditional Irish family; big and noisy. I have eight sisters and amazing parents but sometimes things were scarce; time, money, clothes, physical space, and mental space.

My father was brought up by his mother, as his father, my grandfather, died when my father was a baby. At a young age, he became the man of the house. He was highly self-motivated and very disciplined. He took a job with the Civil Service at eighteen and put himself through college in the evenings.

My mother came from a more privileged background. Her father was a self-made entrepreneur, but he died young and sadly had not made provision for his family through insurance protection policies or something similar. My mother went from being wealthy to having to downsize quite dramatically in a very short space of time.

When she married my father, she was obliged to give up her job as a librarian. In Ireland at this time, married women were not permitted to work in certain jobs. Overnight, she went from being an independent woman with her own income and a job she loved, to being a wife and mother with little or no financial independence.

My mother was very enterprising, but she frequently felt on the back foot when it came to money as she felt she lacked her own financial independence. Some of her entrepreneurial endeavours included writing and publishing a children's Irish vocabulary book, delivering cookery programmes for radio and hosting foreign students.

I suspect I unconsciously modelled her behaviour, although my siblings and I were brought up to be independent and strong-minded women. The unconscious belief that I held was that women stayed at home and/or take care of the home and children and men were the earners and providers. Even though this was not what I was told growing up, sometimes we are unaware of our beliefs and behaviours.

I began full time work at c. nineteen and I met my now ex-husband around the same time. His upbringing had been similar to mine. His parents had similar beliefs. His father worked full time and his mother was a stay at home parent.

We bought a house together, married, and had my incredible son in a fairly short space of time. Shortly after my son was born, things began to deteriorate for many reasons. My story is my story alone and out of respect for the other people mentioned and involved, some of the finer details have been omitted.

At times, my ex-husband would say he would prefer a mother to stay at home and look after the children while he went to work. He wanted a wife and I wanted my life. This was probably one of the many conversations we should have had before we got married. I resisted, not only did I enjoy working, but financially, we needed two incomes coming in. My ex-husband was running his own business, not hugely profitably, so my salary contribution was important to the household.

On paper, I "had it all". I had a husband, a house, a car, a job and a child, but I was very unhappy without really knowing why. To quote my wonderful and now adult son "Mum, do think you might be the problem?" I was-unhappy because I did not know what I really wanted. I had no clarity, no real direction and no BIG WHY. By the way, if your BIG WHY does not make you cry, then it's not big enough.

At that time, I had no clear idea how to manage money, I had a mortgage, and a car finance agreement I did not understand and a husband who I struggled to communicate with. I did not know how to have important conversations, I felt uncomfortable talking about money. I held the belief that talking about money was somehow vulgar. I had no idea how much we owed, how much we earned collectively and no idea how to plan our weekly and monthly outgoings while also make plans for our future stability as a family. To make a long story short, our relationship broke down. We were fortunate to be able to reach a separation agreement through mediation [1].

Suddenly, I was faced with documents and situations I did not understand. I did know how to complete a statement of means or even what it was. This was a wake-up call for me. Although this was many years ago, I felt that renting was not really a sustainable option for my circumstances and I wanted to find another solution. I was guided through the separation process by the mediator. Their job is not to intervene but to help both parties to reach a sustainable solution.

The startling realisation about this process was that it highlighted all the conversations we should have had before we got married. How had I allowed this to happen? Where had it all gone wrong? It stemmed from my unconscious inherited beliefs and also my feelings of a low self-worth. I also needed to let go of the "could have, should have, would have" or "coulda shoulda woulda" for short.

Somewhere along the way, my self-worth and confidence had taken a bit of a hammering. I felt trapped and suffocated. I knew what I did not want and that was where all my focus was being directed. Energy flows where focus goes, and all energy moves increments should this be incrementally or increments. Once energy starts moving, it gains momentum. The more I focused on what I did not want, the more energy I was directing into the areas of my life that were not working.

The definition of insanity is doing the same thing over and over but expecting a different result each time. It took me a long to realise that I was unconsciously repeating the same patterns of behaviour but ironically, I was expecting a different result. I felt I had failed as a wife and a mother. The guilt of not being able to make things work was overwhelming. I felt guilty for breaking up a family, but I feel in reality, two parents that live happily apart are probably better than two parents that live in conflict and stay together for the sake of their children. I had two choices, stay stuck or move forward. In life, you are always advancing or retreating.

> *"Get busy living or get busy dying."*
>
> *- Andy, Shawshank Redemption*

I managed to get my finances and paperwork organised enough to be able to take out a mortgage and buy a property on my own. This was the scariest but most exciting time of my life. I was on my own, it was just me and my son, there was one income coming in and that was mine. I did not have a back-up plan, so I had to make it work. Sometimes, our greatest successes come from when our backs are against the wall. I learned very quickly, through necessity, how to record, track and analyse my expenses. I started out with a notebook and a pen. I now use a cloud-based app on my phone. The actual method does not matter; the action does.

I recorded all my expenses, without judgement and then analysed everything going out at the end of the month. I began to create an awareness of where my money was going. I also started to track all the money that was coming into my life to remind myself that all money is real. I recorded all the money I earned from working, money I found on the ground, discounts I got, vouchers I received, and I also started to record the value of things. If someone bought me lunch, I recorded an approximate value. If I was gifted something, I recorded an approximate value. This step is very important. The reason that most "budgets" [2] fail is that people make very restrictive spending plans without any foundation, instead of using real data that is personal to them to create a flexible personal spending plan. I like the simple philosophy of spend some, save some, give some away, but always pay yourself first.

I also began to look at ways to increase my income. I frequently felt that there was too much month left at the end of the money.

- I negotiated a pay rise at work by making a list of all of my achievements to date, how I felt I was adding value to the company and why I felt I deserved an increase. I asked, believed in myself and received.
- I hosted foreign students.
- I showed houses for sale at the weekends.

These are a small sample of the types of ways you can increase your income. If you earn extra income outside of the *Pay As You*

Earn system, it is your responsibility to declare it to tax office but remember that you may not always incur a tax liability.

I was beginning to put my life back together again and reclaim in my independence and personal power when a new man came into my life. He seemed to be attracted my independence, my inner strength and my sense of determination. Unfortunately, I did not realise at the time that he probably had a low self-worth and was carrying considerable personal debt from poor habits with money. Ironically, he actually felt more comfortable being in debt than having wealth.

I became the "fixer", a self-assumed role of trying to help other people, whether they want to be helped or not. This is very different to coaching where the process is collaborative.

I took over rather than empowered. I renegotiated all his personal debt, had interest rates frozen, fees and charges reversed and had some debts written off. However, the success was soon short lived. His comfort zone was being in debt and his brain did everything in its power to bring him back to that place. The missing piece of the puzzle was that I never involved him in the process and he never actually asked for help in the first place. Not only did he end up in worse debt than when I met him, I also incurred personal debt on his behalf. I had two choices; stay in victim mode or take responsibility, learn from my mistakes and move forward.

I take personal responsibility for this now, although it took me quite a few years to take ownership. I was the one who facilitated the bad behaviour. I was the one who co-signed the loan, the credit card and the finance agreement. I was the one who did not establish clear boundaries regarding what was acceptable and what was absolutely unacceptable.

"Success principle number 1, take responsibility".

- *Jack Canfield, author of the Success Principles.*

The main reason for this financial mess was that I still could not bring myself to have "money conversations" with another person, particularly someone I was romantically involved with. Once again, the relationship broke down but this time around, the break up was like an atomic bomb. The fall out was huge. I was the proud owner of two mortgages and not enough money coming in. We had both been made redundant and the relationship had broken down, leaving me with the financial and mental burden of responsibility. The mortgages were in joint names.

Note: When a loan is in two names, if one person stops paying for whatever reason, the other person is jointly responsible.

We had bought a house together. I had not considered my strategies around "getting in" and "getting out". This does not mean that it is important to keep one eye on the door at all times but for each and every agreement you enter into, it is prudent to get clarity on a few things and ask yourself some reflective questions.

- Why am I doing this?
- What am I getting myself into?
- When will I get out?
- When can I get out?
- Can I get out at all?
- If I want to get out early, can I?
- Are there any penalties if I change my mind or get out early?
- What are the costs – hidden and up front?
- How long will this last?
- Do I fully understand what I am doing?
- Who else in involved?
- Does this agreement fit with my personal values and will it bring me closer to my goal – whatever that goal is.

Not only was I left with substantial mortgage debt, but I was also left with personal debt that I had not incurred but I had facilitated by co-signing a loan and allowing someone else access to my credit card. When I look back on this, I realise that I was facilitating the bad behaviour because I still had a low self-worth. I had tried to buy love. I thought if I bought things for someone else, it would make me feel better about myself. I was afraid to talk about that awkward subject – money. I was afraid to establish my boundaries.

When I finally reclaimed my personal power, it was like a light bulb had gone off in my head. The clouds in my mind cleared. I realised I needed to ask for help and that I could not manage the situation on my own.

"To have it all does not mean you have to do it all."

- *Sharon Lechter, Think and Grow Rich for Women*

I needed a plan of action and these are the steps I followed to bring about my success.

Step 1 - Decide

I decided I was no longer willing to accept my life as it was. I decided to change. I decided what I did not want because then I could focus on Step 2.

Step 2 - Clarity

I decided what I did want and got absolute clarity. I wrote it down using the **Be Do Have** method. I then anchored my goals and desires using physical and visual anchors, journaling, affirmations, afformations. I focused on the *What* and the *Why* and let go of How.

Step 3 - Declutter

I chose to declutter mentally, physically, emotionally and spiritually using my simple formula.

Fit, flatter, function or fill you with joy, fling it out.

If it did not fit me, flatter me, function or fill me with joy, I was going to fling it out. I became ruthless in a good way. As I cleared my physical space, I asked myself, 'Do I want to keep this <object, belief, email, person> in my life?' I deliberately chose to ask if I wanted to keep it rather than asking if I wanted to fling it out, as this felt like a more empowering question to ask myself.

I decluttered my mindset by writing in my journal, any disempowering beliefs and old money memories that were no longer serving me. I sat and meditated for a few minutes and then simply drew a line through them. I released and let go. Decluttering allowed me to make mental and physical space in my life. It also helped reduce my outgoings considerably. I decluttered recurring subscriptions I was no longer using and bank charges I did not need to pay. I also decluttered my language. I stopped using disempowering words and expressions, particularly around money. I used my Neuro Linguistic Programme techniques to come up with more empowering ways of saying things.

I stopped saying "I can't afford that" and instead I said, "I am choosing to spend my money in alignment with my values, goals and personal spending plan".

I spent money virtually. I would check my bank balance and "spend" the balance over and over on things I wanted to have and do. This encouraged my mind to expand what I felt was possible and it's a fun exercise to do anyway.

Step 4 - Discover your BIG WHY

I needed leverage on myself. I needed a reason bigger than myself to motivate me into action. My BIG WHY has and always will be my family. When things became difficult and I wanted to give up, I gently reminded myself of my higher motivation and kept going.

Step 5 - Establish clear boundaries

Set clear boundaries with your family, friends, clients and anyone else in your life. It is up to you to decide and also communicate what is acceptable and what is not. We are the measure of the 5 people we spend most time with. Choose those people wisely and associate with people that share and support your beliefs and goals.

"Nice girls don't get the corner office"

- Lois Frankel

I became mindful as to how I was treating myself and how I was speaking to myself. I began to love, honour and respect myself and guess what, so did other people because I was no longer willing to settle for less. This does not mean that I'm inflexible or unaccommodating, although my son would disagree. It simply means that I value myself above all else, I put myself first, pay myself first and love myself first because if I don't, no one else will.

I consciously chose to declutter any blame and shame I was carrying around. I chose to stop blaming other people for my mistakes. I chose to stop blaming myself for allowing myself to have been manipulated and used. I chose to stop blaming myself for not being able to articulate what I needed and what I felt was unacceptable behaviour. I now know that asking for help is a sign of strength, not weakness. It is empowering to face your fears head on and stare them down. When you face your fears, they no longer have power over you. As I did not know where to start, I typed "mortgage debt help" into *Google* and hoped for the best.

I made contact with MABS, a free government funded Money Advice and Budgeting Service in Ireland. I was able to negotiate a moratorium, which is like a mortgage holiday, on both mortgages. Basically, I was able to suspend payments for a few months while I drew breath. Being honest with myself for the first time in years felt refreshing and liberating. Once again, I need to figure out where I was and where I wanted to go and let go of how I was going to get there. I got leverage on myself by focusing on my BIG WHY. The reason most people do not get what they want in life, is because they don't have clarity. See Step 2 above.

The mortgage moratorium did not mean that the money owed "went away". It was added on to the end of my mortgage plus interest. This is important to note. I had a less than ideal credit rating for five years after the final mortgage payment was cleared. This situation was a bit challenging for a while but liberating because I began with the end in mind. Not only did I have need to rebuild my credit history, but I needed to rebuild my life and my self-esteem.

Always know more about yourself than the other person, where possible. You can request a copy of your credit report for free or a small charge from your local credit bureau or registration agency, depending on which country you live in. It is a useful exercise to monitor your own credit rating.

I began to realise that success leaves clues. If I wanted a life of financial freedom, I needed to model the behaviour of people who had already achieved what I wanted and do the same. I started to read every personal development and financial empowerment book I could find. The underlying principles were to focus on what is already positive in your life and acknowledge that, get clarity and pay yourself first.

I began a practice of daily gratitude. I started to "book end" my day. I would start my morning by journaling and deciding how I wanted my day to go. This would rarely take me more than a few minutes, but the exercise is very powerful.

I began to design my ideal day asking myself questions such as:

- Who am I with?
- Where am I?
- What can I see, hear, feel, smell, taste, touch?
- How am I earning money?
- How much money am I earning?
- How am I spending my time?
- Where do I live?
- How am I contributing in a positive way to other people?

At the end of the day, I would be thankful for 10 things, events, or people in my life. I chose 10 things, as this was easy to count on my fingers. I still engage in this practice today.

- Thank you for my lovely family.
- Thank you having the strength to ask for help and getting it.
- Thank you for finding coins on the ground today.

And so on.

Many of us focus on what we want to have rather than what we want to be or do. Many people operate with the belief system that if they do what they need to do, they will get what they want to have and then they will be the person they desire to be. That's the Do, Have, Be strategy that rarely works. I researched how I could turn this model upside down.

In order for me to have certain things, I need to be a specific type of person and take certain actions. I began to think that if I acted as my goal had already been achieved, my mind-set would follow. The person I was, was not going to think, act and behave in a way that was going to bring me to my end goal of financial freedom and empowerment. I needed to change the process.

The Be Do Have method of goal setting

I need to **Be** the person I want to be, if I already had achieved my goal, then I would **Do** the things that a successful person would do, which allows me to **Have** exactly what I want.

For example:

I want to have a passive, residual, continuous income that continues, whether or not I get out of bed. In order for that to happen, I need to be proactive and explore opportunities to make this happen. I can visualize until the cows come home but at some point, I need to take inspired action.

I decided I wanted to be an Amazon bestselling author. I needed to take action and actually start writing and look for opportunities to collaborate and create powerful partnerships with other people that could help me make this happen. These inspired actions have allowed me to have a presence on Amazon Kindle as a bestselling co-author. My next big leap is to sign a publishing contract with a well-known publishing house.

For each heading, I decided to come up with 10 things I wanted to **Be**

1. Be a bestselling author
2. Be a good mother

3. Be fit, healthy, confident
4. Be successful in business and my career
5. Be a successful, wealthy investor
6. Be an inspiration to other women
7. Be a homeowner
8. Be a great friend and mentor
9. Be a loving, supportive wife to a wonderful man who will support me also
10. Be the best version of me every single day

I then focused on 10 things I wanted to **Do**.

1. Write several bestsellers and go on an international, all expenses paid book tour.
2. Travel to New Zealand and drive around both islands in a camper van
3. Coach women to achieve financial freedom.
4. Find and marry my soulmate
5. Successfully complete a Masters degree
6. Successfully complete a fully funded PhD programme
7. Collaborate with incredible successful people that inspire me every day

8. Learn to drive an ambulance - why not?
9. Smash my six-figure income goal
10. Complete a full marathon - I never said "run".

My **Have** list is something like this

1. Have a lucrative publishing contract with a well-known publishing agency matching my values like Hay House, that allows me to continue writing inspirational books for women.
2. Have a beautiful energy efficient home in a quiet location with a landscaped garden and space for all my family (and all their clutter) and an ENORMOUS utility room with drying facilities.
3. Have a personal assistant that looks after day to day administration stuff, keeps me on track with appointments and acts as a gatekeeper.
4. Have a housekeeper that looks after our lovely energy efficient home, keeps it clean, does laundry, runs errands and keeps my family fed and nourished with healthy food.
5. Have a *Dyson* hair dryer - who does not want to go from Side Show Bob to sleek and smooth in twenty-two seconds or less?

6. Have a personal stylist that know what clothes suit me and helps me find the right outfit for every occasion, that will compliment my great hair.
7. Have a fully furnished "girl cave" in our lovely home, with space for me to see clients, hide out, meditate, chill, read and escape the clutter of my husband and my son.
8. Have a personal trainer that whips me into physical shape and keeps me there.
9. Have a business coach that will call me out on my own limiting beliefs and help me set and exceed every goal I set myself.
10. Have and drive a Jaguar XF in burgundy with a cream leather interior. I would not say no to having a driver.

I decided to use a combination of *affirmations* and *afformations* ©Noah St John. An affirmation is a positive statement as a reminder to your unconscious mind of a specific goal that you would like to achieve. It normally starts with "I am", e.g., "I am healthy, wealthy, loved, whole and complete."

My own personal favourite is "I am open and willing to receive the daily abundance of money that flows to me easily, effortlessly and from everywhere". I still use this affirmation daily but one of the problems with affirmations is that your brain can retaliate and say, "Liar Liar pants on fire".

An afformation puts a slightly different slant on an affirmation and asks a question so your brain has to search to find a solution. Remember, there are always solutions; you just need to find them.

"Why does a daily abundance flow to me easily, effortlessly and from everywhere?" "Why am I so lucky?"

Noah St John suggests starting your questions with *Why?* It puts your brain into enquiry mode. Think of your brain like *Google* or an internet search engine. Using a combination of affirmations and afformations will help you bridge what is known as the "belief gap". This is the space between your current perceived reality and your new desired reality. Note the word "perceived". To perceive something is to understand it or to come to realise. We can change our perception by changing our mind-set and create a new desired reality.

Studies have shown that while the conscious mind can hold only a few ideas at a time, your subconscious mind can hold many more. I tell my son that if he wants me to remember something, I might have to delete something else important, like his birthday, so he needs to choose wisely what he would like me to remember. You can never really overwhelm your subconscious mind, no matter how hard you try. These techniques are simple, easy and do not cost anything. The only investment is your time.

I normally work with a few affirmations and afformations at any one time. I'll write them down on *Post Its* and stick them all over my house and car. I'll put them on the inside of my cupboards, sometimes unconsciously, so I cannot NOT see them. I also write them down several times a day as part of my daily journaling as this means I am engaging with my brain on an emotional and physical level when my pen makes contact with the paper. Sometimes I record myself speaking into my phone and play it back to myself when I'm out for a walk.

I also use visual and physical anchors, as I mentioned earlier. A visual anchor is an image or representation of something I want to achieve. It helps me to align myself with positive energy. I use a cardboard 1,000,000 euro note as a book marker. I make vision boards or dream boards using images cut from magazines of things and goals I want to achieve and look at them every day. I usually take a photograph of my current vision board and use it as wallpaper on my computer, tablet and mobile phone. I set up reminders on my phone that pop up randomly saying things like

"Congratulations on your new book deal". My son gave me a *Swarovski* pen for my birthday. Every time I use it, I say to myself "This is the type of pen a wealthy woman uses". Every time I look in the mirror, regardless of how I look, I say "This is what a wealthy woman looks like".

I also ask myself "Do my current actions match my current goals?".

This technique uses the power of advertising on myself and to my own advantage.

"What's the difference between a millionaire and a billionaire? The billionaire writes HER goals down twice a day."

- *Source Unknown*

I firmly believe that there is no "one size fits all" solution. I used and still use a combination of techniques to get myself out debt and start building wealth. The specific method does not really matter, the inspired action does. So, what next? I love making life easy for myself. If it's not easy, I'm not doing it. Simply follow the steps below to manifest your dream life and reclaim your power. The Universe loves speed or more simply put, there is power in momentum so let's get started.

1. Decide that you want to change and share your goal with someone you trust and who will inspire you along the way.
2. Decide what you want, write it down and review it daily. Face your fears and take action.
   FEAR = Focused Effort + Action = Results
3. Know where you are now by figuring out how much you have, how much you owe, how much you are spending and how much is coming in.
4. Make a personal spending plan and spend your money in accordance with your plan and NOT your bank balance.
5. Declutter as if your life depended on it and that includes people, beliefs and physical stuff. Declutter any money memories that you feel are holding you back.
6. Focus on the what and the why and let go of the how. If your BIG WHY does not make you cry, it's probably not big enough.
7. Create anchors to align yourself with your goals.
8. Make gratitude part of your daily practice. I live my life with an attitude of gratitude every day.

"The question is not at what age I want to retire, it's at what income."

- *George Forema*

[1] This option is free, considerably less stressful and more sustainable.

[2] I personally hate the term "budget" and I prefer to use "personal spending plan".

Some of my favourite empowering books for women

Nice Girls Don't Get The Corner Office - Lois P Frankel

The Wealth Chef - Ann Wilson

The Confidence to Succeed - Donna Kennedy

Making a Living Without a Job - Barbara Winter

Think and Grow Rich for Women - Sharon Lechter

The Success Principles - Jack Canfield

The Book of Afformations - Noah St John

Activate Your Life - Derek Loudermilk, co-authored by Aoife Gaffney

Financial Freedom Explained, Third Edition, co-authored by Aoife Gaffney

Courage
by Martina O'Riordan

Hello, I'm Martina O'Riordan, owner of MartinaO Weddings and Events (www.martinao.com). In this book I would like to share my story with you so that you can be confident that no matter what you want in life, it is possible. With the right attitude and the right plan, you can make your goals a reality.

If you told me ten years ago, or even five years ago that I would set up my own business one day, I would never have believed you! I would never have believed that I would have the courage to go out on my own and take such a risk, but I did. I want to share my story with you, in the hope that it will encourage you to achieve what you want. If you have an idea or goal, but you don't feel like you are ready to implement or take action on it yet, I am hoping this will help you put a plan of action in place and help you believe in yourself and your abilities to make it happen. It's important for you to understand that, in my opinion, achieving a goal it not about taking a huge leap into the unknown, it is about preparing yourself and putting a solid plan in place, so you naturally transition into your goal.

In hindsight, I can see how the last few years were preparation in some ways and I was laying the foundations unknowingly to setting up my business MartinaO. The foundations and the silent preparations that I was unaware of at the time were really about giving me the courage and equipping me with the skills to take the leap.

I studied Business and Accounting in university and was one of those people that really didn't know what I wanted to do. Throughout my degree, I thought perhaps I wanted to get into HR because I enjoyed working with people, but then I thought about the fact that I am quite creative, so maybe I should do marketing, and this back and forth list continued. I feel it is such a difficult decision to have to make when you are in school, to decide what you want to do long-term, essentially what you want to be when you grow up. Well that journey from leaving school to deciding I wanted to set up the business took me almost fifteen years. Some people know straight away what they want to do and feel confident to do it, but I was one of those people that really didn't know and spent a lot of time figuring that out.

I was lucky to work with some fabulous companies like *Google* and *Pfizer* early on and through these different opportunities, I began to understand what I enjoyed and what I didn't enjoy. Organising events (no surprise there!) became a part of my early roles and I really began to enjoy this aspect of the job. This early exposure to events and marketing was to have a massive impact on my future business and career! By then I was really eager to continue growing in the Corporate world and as the recession hit in Ireland, I knew that a promotion or step-up would be put on hold, as there was so much uncertainty, and I didn't want to wait. I started thinking about how I could keep progressing and it became clear that I needed to go abroad. Thinking about the prospect made me a little nervous but it was a choice I felt I needed to make, if I was to progress. And so, I decided to move to Australia to further my career and of course my life experiences. It is here that I think it's important for you to know, I did not just take one big leap into the unknown. I prepared myself and I created a plan. I made the decision to research what life in Australia would be like, and once I was assured there would not be snakes circling the main streets of Sydney, I felt comfortable enough to head off. Really, through my preparation, I was ensuring I would survive. I am sure many people don't go through this step of doing lots of research, but I wanted to know what I was getting into so that I could be prepared. I suppose that is the natural planner in me, and of course I got working on the spreadsheet to equip myself with the knowledge I needed before going. I have always found that preparation minimises the number of surprises that you can have and will enable you to be prepared should something happen. This also helps with any fear that you have of course, because you have a little bit more of an insight into what you are about to leap in to.

Whilst in Australia I was very lucky to get a role with Global company, *Bupa*. As I progressed as a Senior Leader within the business, a lot of time was invested in me and my career trajectory. At the time, I was Corporate Events Manager and I really enjoyed the creativity that came with organising events. Being a natural planner, I was very systematic with my approach to ensure nothing went wrong and there was always a backup. I got to travel all over Australia organising events, I was very lucky. As my role evolved into many other fascinating projects, I really began to miss the number of events I was previously working on. It might have been in a personal development meeting where my manager asked me had I ever thought about setting up my own events company. What a lightbulb moment that was! Maybe I had thought about it before, but for someone to believe that I could do it, well that was a whole new story.

I began to toy with the notion of setting up my own Wedding & Events Business. I had an area of expertise and I wanted that to be of benefit to other people. Though I loved the corporate events, I wanted to really let the creative juices flow and use my expertise to help people and couples create their dream day. And that essentially became the reason I set up my business, I wanted to help people. I knew I was good at planning, and so I got to work, putting the plan together, ironically!

I started mapping out the journey of what it would take to get there, and I had some tough decisions to make. I also had the fear playing in the back of my mind as to whether I would be capable of setting up my own business. Sometimes we can be our own worst enemies. Knowing in the back of my mind the positive experiences created through events and weddings was my drive to not let the fear take over. I often think the fear is what drives us all to plan that little bit extra, and to be that little bit more organised, but drive and "the why" energises us to do it.

As part of my business planning, I first had to decide if I would set up in Australia or move back to Ireland. Though I loved Australia, and still do, Ireland is my home and I am truly passionate about our country, its quirks and the amazing landscape. Before I left Ireland, I had wanted to work in tourism promoting our country to foreign visitors. This I guess made the decision a little bit easier, I wanted to promote our country to people outside of Ireland to get married here. I wanted to promote all that Ireland has to offer, and I wanted to show them a real Irish experience. So, this became Step 1, I was moving home!

Now there were many pieces of the puzzle coming together at the one time. I then started looking at what was needed to set up a business. I decided to undergo a Diploma in Weddings & Events so that I could have a formal qualification in this area. I had worked in the area for many years, but I thought it would be something interesting to do and may help to reassure me that I was making the right decision. The Diploma took two years and it really helped to lay down the foundations and it did just as I was hoping. It reaffirmed my love for Weddings & Events. I truly enjoyed it. Not every minute of course, it was difficult to go back studying after being a long time out of university. I studied whilst making the transition back home from Australia and whilst working full time.

Once I moved home, I spent time thinking about how I would get into the Industry here in Ireland. As I had been gone for so long from Ireland, I had lost a lot of my connections and contacts. I decided that working in a hotel would be a great way to connect with people in the industry, easy peasy right? Wrong! I hadn't worked in a hotel before which made that step a little more difficult than I had expected. I thought I might have been snapped up with my experience but of course the reality was a little bit different. Good old expectations eh! I didn't have too long to wait before I got a position as Wedding & Events Coordinator in a hotel and this gave me great exposure to the industry in Ireland, but not only that, it gave me exposure to some fabulous couples.

Whilst I was working in the hotel, I started to put the other pieces of the puzzle together. I underwent a Start Your Own Business course with my Local Enterprise Office. Though I was passionate about planning weddings and events, I hadn't a clue about setting up my own business and, as you know, the unknown can be daunting. However, I went with it. This course really catapulted me forward and made me realise that I was really doing this! The course helped me with the business steps like registering the business, finalising the business plan, formulating your marketing plan etc; and then I started building the website. The more I learned, the more confident I became. This was all happening in the background and I was lucky enough to be able to go part time in my role in the hotel, to allow me to further focus on the business. In a way, the hotel was a safety net. It allowed me to get geared up for full time MartinaO, but it also made me realise that this is truly what I wanted to do. Seeing the couples I was helping on their journeys is exactly why I was setting up. Knowing I could help them, and knowing how much it enhanced their day, kept me going. It was a long process and many long hours. Each day, I would finish work, drive over an hour to get home, and immediately start working on MartinaO. As I mentioned, being able to do this and being able to work part time was a little safety net while setting up, it was buying me time. Do you have a safety net that could make things a little bit easier for you? My safety net made me feel like I was dipping my toe in the water and testing it out. You don't have to leap, but make sure you move! And of course, with anything the time comes when you must let go.

Since that time, I haven't looked back, nor had I known what to really expect. I don't think you can ever truly understand what is ahead of you because every business is different, and everyone's journey is different. I have loved every minute of it, but it has been very challenging. Getting the first few bookings under the brand of MartinaO was so exciting and seeing those play out was utterly rewarding. To receive the emails, texts and cards of gratitude are all things that put more fuel in the fire that keeps me motivated. The first year was a whirlwind. I worked extremely hard and was absolutely thrilled to feature in Vogue. If you had told me at the start of the business when I was still full of doubt and fear that I would feature in *Vogue* in Year 1, I would have laughed.

I mentioned fear and doubt earlier, and this is normal, just don't let it consume you. This is what can easily hold you back from doing what you really want to do. Write your idea down and start mind mapping (writing your goal in the middle and writing everything that pops to mind about that goal around it) it so that you can start formulating the plan. I feel it is also important to write those doubts down. Like anyone, one of my fears is the fear of failure, and a whole pile of 'what if's' that go with it, but I also don't believe in having regrets. If I hadn't set up the business, I would forever wonder would I have been able to do it, and what would it have looked like. To some people it probably seemed like I had suddenly set up a business, but those that were around me would have seen the years of planning and preparation that went into it. I did spend some time thinking about what failure could look like so that I was being realistic, but I also think perhaps you don't really understand what failure is until you get there. All you can do is really prepare to ensure you put your best foot forward and hopefully not get to the failing stage. I am still not sure what failure would look like. I feel I have learnt so much throughout the process and met so many amazing people that I am already winning, and those experiences cannot be taken away. I am living my why.

One thing that I learned in Australia was to not worry so much about what other people think. Yes, I went to Australia to learn that! Setting up a business throws you out into the limelight whether you want to be out there or not, and it will be very difficult to succeed if you spend your time focusing on what other people are thinking about you, rather than focusing on your marketing plan for example. People will have opinions no matter what, and sometimes you have to go with your gut and do what you think is right for you and block out some of the opinions that fill you with more doubt, rather than encourage you to go on.

Through all the doubts and the fear, the opinions and the preparation, you also have to spend time visualising your goal as a big success. Yes, I am a believer in the vision board (placing pictures in front of you so you have visual reminders of what you want) and mapping out what happiness means for you. Spend time thinking about and allowing yourself to feel the emotions that could come with achieving *your* goal. That feeling will give you the drive to keep going. And on the days of doubt that pop up after you have launched your goal (and yes you will have them!), use that vision board, visualising what success looks like and go back to your plan, this will help keep you on track.

A helpful tool I used when dabbling with the idea of setting up my business was writing the pro's and con's list. This allows you to think about 'What is the worst that can happen?' and compare it to 'What is the best that can happen?'. When you see the positives outweigh the negatives that will reassure the decision you have made, and again will add fuel to the fire. It will keep you motivated. That fire, your why, is the thing that pushes you and gets you to take action and do the thing you have been putting off. Your inner strength isn't something I think you can just look for and once you find it, off you go. I believe it is a culmination of things that drive you to do what you want to do. My inner strength along the way came from some of the following feelings or actions; absolutely loving the Diploma in Weddings & Events, seeing the positive impact that I can have on someone's wedding day, visualising how successful my business can be, the cards of thanks and of course being able to use my expertise to help other people, which is why I set up the business in the first place. These are the things that give me the drive to keep going. What do you think spurs you on? With the idea that you are dabbling with at the moment, do you have a list of actions that could lead to that positive feeling that will motivate you to keep going? Perhaps take some time to write down your thoughts.

If you decide to make the move to setting up a business or whatever it is you have been thinking about doing, you need to know what drives you and you need to be able to recognise the little signs throughout the process that reaffirm you have made the right decision. Listening to and understanding your gut is crucial throughout the process and when you break it down, if you set yourself up with a plan so that you are taking baby steps rather than throwing yourself in at the deep end, it makes it that little bit easier. There are of course some people that just throw themselves in head first and I think that is enviable, but I am definitely not one of those people! I am a planner and a lover of a good spreadsheet!

So, has it been a success or not? If I look at why I set up in the first place, it was to use my expertise to help other people. Has it worked? Yes. I have been able to really help people that need it and enhance the experience for them and their guests, on their wedding day. I work with all sorts of couples from high profile to busy professionals and knowing that I can support them and enable them to have their dream day makes it worthwhile. My favourite moment is on the day, usually during the ceremony (when I get to see it!), and they are exchanging vows. I see the emotion in their faces, the nerves have vanished and often it seems like it is just the two of them in the room. To see the love and knowing that I have played a small part in getting them to this stage, and seeing the happy faces of not only them, but their guests, this makes it worthwhile for me. This is my Why.

Make your goal worthwhile for you. And have courage to start today. You are capable!

Happiness and Gratitude
by Maria Farrell

If you're not happy, then make the change. You deserve to be happy!

I believe that when you find happiness within yourself the rest will follow, and it's important that you find that inner strength, so you can be the best version of yourself. Do not rely on someone or something else to make you happy or validate your contribution to the world. You are already enough and there is no one like you and there never will be. You my friend are unique. To compare yourself to others or seek happiness outside of yourself is an insult to the people who brought you into the world.

I truly think that we have all been guilty of taking that big criticism stick out from time to time to emotionally beat ourselves up and try to dampen our sparkle, unconsciously or consciously. Lots of times, especially in times of despair, I found myself doing just that. I looked for answers to happiness. I questioned where I could find it. 'Where do I go to find it? When is it coming? What do I need to do to find it? What am I doing wrong?'

There were many dark days in my journey and I carried a heavy heart at certain times, but I found the strength, I dug deep and reminded myself frequently that two wonderful people brought me into this world to be happy, not just to make do. Awareness is key. In the past I entertained that negative critical voice. Once I became aware of what I was doing, I reframed it and chose to do something different. I now refer to that critical voice as "The Menacing Little Shite" and if it comes to town, I tell him there's no time to talk. Instead of engaging with it, I simply notice it, acknowledge it and let it move right along. I think of a loved one or a great memory or see something I'm grateful for.

Being grateful is a vital key to a great life. Even the simplest things will lead you into a mindset that things will seem better. Life becomes more achievable and using small steps, especially if you feel you are in a dark place. One slight change in thought in the right direction can create a whole new result.

In life I give gratitude daily, I say at least ten things I'm grateful very day. I was encouraged by my mentor Donna Kennedy, AKA "Do a Kindness."

Seeing the simplest things in life and giving gratitude prevents us becoming robot-like in a busy life of societal expectation. I have learned the hard way and I have learned that living in the moment will serve you well and make life so much easier. Think of a scenario, say a week ago, a month ago, or a year ago, and think back to a time you wasted on crossing unnecessary bridges and wasting energy on what never was. Ask yourself if it might serve you better to deal with things as they come and reserve your energy for what's necessary, not wasting it on the unnecessary. I work on this daily and, as I've got cute at it, I've realised that I'm in the driving seat of my life.

What makes you happy? If you don't know, at least become open to finding out. There's a fine line of what makes you happy or what makes others happy. If you are already happy, I'm buzzing for you! May it continue. If you are not happy, ask yourself what's not making you happy and what would make you happy. If you have an unfulfilling yearning for something, follow your gut instinct as this, right now, is your time. Now is your journey and your chance to make a change and a difference in the world, no matter how little or how large, it's yours!

Everybody's journey is so different, and we all have our part to play. It's never too late. Start today in this minute. Make a solemn vow to yourself that you are going to be the happiest version of yourself. Do this live in the moment and take one day at a time and see what makes you glow and feel alive. Happiness is not about being perfect, it's about feeling uplifted, at peace and being the true version of who you are. Happiness can come in many ways as we all know. For me it's a smile and a laugh from loved ones, the smell of my horse's coat and the way he kisses me, the way my dog greets me every day, as if it was all her birthdays wrapped up in one. Focus on what makes you feel happy.

Acceptance of yourself as a truly magnificent human being, an individual that no comparison need apply. Your light is as bright as anyone else's so please do me and yourself a favour and stop covering it up and giving others the authority to dampen it down. Shine bright as you possibly can by simply being your wonderful self, warts and all!

Accepting Yourself

I fought with myself for a very long time, comparing myself in lots of ways in my life at all ages. It's the most toxic thing you can ever do to yourself and it only produces heartache and barriers, which is such a waste of time. I believe shite happens but it's how you deal with it and how can you grow from it that matters.

You must love yourself first, as you would love someone else. Imagine getting that emotional stick out to someone you love and beating them with it, telling them they are not good enough, beautiful enough, famous enough, wealthy enough. Would you do that to someone else? Why do it to yourself? STOP IT NOW! Be kind to yourself, as you would be to someone else. Protect yourself, nurture yourself and be grateful that you've such an amazing light inside of you. Most of us are blessed with two arms so do the most important thing and put your two arms around yourself and embrace yourself with love. Go on, try it now. That didn't hurt, did it? If you don't have arms, improvise and imagine it or get someone else to put their arms around you.

"I'm never going to let your negative vibes and comments get through to my psyche and cripple me"

- Damien Dempsey, Irish Folk Singer

It's simpler than you think to apply this as it's within you naturally and it always has been, you've just been brain washed by society, circumstances and others' opinions. It's time to set your own true principles in life and you will see how you evolve into the real you.

Peace of Mind

Society, social media, advertising etc. can very easily have an adverse effect on our own outlook in life, if we let it. It challenges us on how we seemingly should act or seemingly how we should look. One word... rubbish! Be comfortable with where you want to go, who you want to be around and ask yourself, if are you at ease with this. Does it uplift you or pull you down and maybe make you feel uncomfortable? If it makes you unhappy, then you may have to make a few changes by listening quietly to yourself. You should never be made to feel inferior to anyone. As the saying goes, find your tribe that will gladly help and love to see you shine.

I want to tell you how I accepted myself. I took down all the barriers that I had built around myself over the years. What I looked for was peace of mind and to be at one with myself. I slowed down in my social life and hung out with those that only uplifted me and that I dearly love. I took a few years out to see a new way, which I'm still learning and developing every day, by the way. I asked myself questions that I had never asked before and at times I didn't like the answers I came up with, but I started getting more clarity and I found myself again - the real Maria came to the surface.

At this point, I would like to tell you about my life journey so far so you can see why self-acceptance is so importance to happiness.

I had a happy childhood. I have six siblings and love them all. My mum and dad were amazing parents but sadly my mum passed away several years ago with leukaemia. I miss her every day, but I know she lives on in me and mine. My parents made me who I am today and thankfully I still have my dad, Jackie Farrell, who is a legend and the most amazing dad and friend. I think I got both their strengths. Growing up I was a force to be reckoned with and I had very big ideas. Dad once said I used to ask to do something after I had it done. I've always had a big connection to horses, although we couldn't afford a horse. As a family we wanted for nothing. We had a home and we had our family holidays - a horse was not a necessity, although it still didn't stop me from popping notes and letters throughout the house yearly requesting one! I started to ride other people's ponies and I had wildness in me and loved to gallop. I hated putting saddles on and my feet in stirrups then as the wilder and freer the better. I then got good and started show jumping and loved it and done well. But there was a time in my younger years a man non related to me that tried to take advantage of my love for horses and use them to ruin my life and my childhood so I quickly changed the predictable outcome very quickly and stopped being in his company and I made a vow I wouldn't share this to save my parents any pain.

I moved forward and enjoyed the show jumping, which helped me, and I grew up quickly. I still love my horses. I also love dogs and I am now a dog trainer by trade. I love making a difference to both the dogs' lives and their owners. I also teach kids how to train their dogs and I'm just about to start up a major new exciting venture.

Through my journey in life I have had two beautiful daughters, Taylor and Beth, whom I adore. They are my legacy in life and they have helped carry me through many tough times, even though they are probably not aware of it. I experienced several challenges and tough times, but I have got through them. I have two broken marriages, but I regret nothing. For all the things that life has taught me, I am extremely grateful and yes, even though I was in dark places many times, I rose again to open the next chapter. As I stand today, I have been in a relationship for several years with the love of my life, who I adore. We met after I did a bit of soul searching. We met at the races, so yes horses were never ever too far away! I am happy and grateful for my journey so far and look forward to seeing what else I need to learn in life.

I had a choice from a very young age to let things affect me. Having had challenges, I could take on the label of victim, but I was not going to have that label. I have peace of mind of all the negative, hurtful and malicious things that were done or said to me or behind my back and I wouldn't change a thing as I am everything you see today, and I can still smile and grow stronger daily. I am amazing and so are you!

When you practise this daily just see how you draw in harmony and peace and a grounding transformation takes place. Having a healthy beautiful peace of mind and calmness is heavenly and rewarding.

Prepare to make choices

Being true to yourself will help you sit more comfortably in your own life and open new experiences and know you're on the right path and I feel gives you more strength to help others also. I have made choices in my life that were not true to me. By doing this they came back to bite me on the bum - bloody sore too! If I was more aware at certain times and had the strength, I may not have had the hardship I endured and yet part of me wouldn't change a thing as it has enlightened me so much. It's when you don't learn something from an event that brings more hardship.

Everyone has their own unique journey and making mistakes isn't a bad thing. We always have choices and sometimes choices aren't easy. We may prefer to take a less stressful choice at the time, going against our gut possibly, but don't be hard on yourself. You made your choices up to now, you can't change them, but you can make new choices, even if it's difficult.

Maintaining peace of mind can take work but it's worth it. I now get up with intention and this might be something you'd like to try also.

I was once told this by the legend that is my Dad to always keep a bit of energy in reserve for myself, so if life gets tough, I can deal with it. Thankfully, I did this and to this day I make a point of holding a little bit back for myself, but still loving my loved ones. By doing this I could make better choices, I was fit to overcome any obstacles that were thrown my way, and I could help others to do the same. It's certainly served me well, so Thank you Dad, you've made me a tough little cookie!

Overall what helped give me peace of mind was making decisions that I knew if I didn't make, somewhere down the line it would have an impact. I've made mistakes and I've made wonderful decisions and yet it's been a rocky road, and at times and scary, but I knew I needed to be courageous and only I could do it and had to dig deep in that reserve tank to receive the better outcome long term. I took a gamble and I won as my life journey has brought me to you today, writing to you my friend, and it has brought me so much more than I ever expected and I know from the bottom of my heart the choices I have made and the life challenges I've endured so far have served me well, after all.

YOU are Enough

Although I loved my late Mummy so much, I was known to be a Daddy's girl. Even though I was highly spirited, out of all my siblings, he always tried to understand me and see my point of view. I will always love him for that as he let me be me. My Mum and Dad taught us all to have good values, and manners were always necessary, although not always carried out by me, if someone was rude to me. They taught me to speak to others as I'd like to be spoken to. My Dad said, "You are no better than anyone in this world and you are no worse than anyone in this world." When I found myself in various situations in life, especially if I felt out of my depth or didn't feel I fitted in, I reminded myself of this, 'They all farted, ate, slept and showered the same as me, although my farts are flower scented, lilies to be exact', so, in fact it became very clear I have my own presence and I didn't need to fit in. I could accept myself as me. I'm so very grateful to you Mum and Dad for all you have done for me, thank you!

The horrible maths teacher

I was only thirteen years old and for some apparent reason she didn't like me…ring a bell to anyone? I have no idea why she was teaching, as she was always so quick tempered and never showed a lot of compassion for anyone and certainly not Miss Maria, as she used to call me. One loved giving Miss Maria a good old dressing down at every opportunity. It didn't go unmissed with other girls in class. I think they felt sorry for me. Well, this particular day, I didn't do my homework as I had a horse show coming up and I needed to practise my double jumps. Hanging on for dear life galloping around a field took it out of me and that night I fell asleep. Not thinking she had me up to the black board the day before to demonstrate my previous night's maths homework, I thought I might get away with it. Well as sure as I thankfully have hair on my head, she called Miss Maria to the board and I felt the blood draining from me. If my leg had of been long enough, I would've kicked my own arse. So up I went, tail between my legs, and had to explain I didn't get it done. That's all the ammunition she needed! She grabbed the ruler and asked me to hold out my hands and I made the decision then and there she wasn't going to lay a finger on me. As we all know there were lots of teachers then that did this, but something changed in me and I wasn't having any of it as it certainly wasn't the first time. I took to my heels and grabbed my bag and told her I had enough, and I wouldn't be back. I marched up to principles office and told her I wanted to be moved to another class. My parents never knew any of this. That day I was frightened and shaking but something else took over and I valued myself enough to say I had enough and, if this carried on, there was only one me. I changed class and I got a kind teacher that listened to children and had respect for human beings. She could also have a bit of banter every now and again, without children feeling threatened or intimidated. Rumour has it, after that, the old maths teacher got married, and she even smiled once. Bless you and thank you for your lesson in life and making me a stronger woman.

You see, we deserve the best and there's only going to be ever one wonderful you and one of me (thank god). I want you to be happy so try this and write a list of things that make you happy and do more of them. You will be more inclined to improve your life in other aspects when you take the time for the things you enjoy.

As mad as it may seem, I sometimes imagine if the first thing we did when meeting somebody new was to close our eyes and listen to their talk and attitude towards life and others, we could truly see their inner being more. I'm a great believer that you don't need to be a sheep and maybe unconsciously lose your identity slightly and get lost in the rat race. Be the shepherdess!

Simple Things

If I'm feeling a bit low or lost, I like to get out into the fresh air and it costs me nothing. As I said, I believe the simple things in life are the most important. In today's world and society we see fancy cars, phones, houses, clothes, etc. Now I love nice things just as much as the next person, and I wish abundance for all and myself, but I never would like to lose myself in material things. You see, to me the world is very badly divided. I recently watched a true story on TV that had a big impact on me, in this sense. In the story, there was a girl called Anna, she was a remarkable brave lady and thankfully lived to tell her story of been trafficked by men against her will. She told her story to help other women that were still being subjected to this cave man behaviour. Her voice was gladly heard in Stormont, and she got a new antislavery act brought in, after they heard her heartfelt horrendous story. Now the reason why I tell you Anna's story is its sometimes until you hit rock bottom, which I most certainly did at one point in my life, it's then that you only have the simple things in life to lift you and embrace. I love the small simple things in life and I like to keep myself grounded to never forget that. Anna just wanted simple freedom. She moved from Romania and was studying to be a nurse in London. She also worked as a cleaner. She was abducted by people that knew her, people from her own country, and sold to traffickers in Ireland for €30,000. She was raped continuously, and mentally, physically and emotionally abused by her persecutors and her mum back home was used as emotional blackmail. The gangs rotated in Belfast, Dublin, Cork and Galway areas. As they kept her passport, she had no way out. I'm telling you this as I want to explain how I see things and hope you understand or maybe relate to the fact that when things are tough, and we don't see a way forward, it can be a very lonely world, even when surrounded by others, but in those times we find hope in the simple things. The simple things can be sometimes the best riches of all. Those walks in the country, that first smile from your child, the sun in your face, the smell of the salt water while walking the beach and hearing the water crash up along the rocks and leaving the effect of white horses with long white flowing manes cruise the sea. Find your simple meaningful things and your life will change for the better.

I was in a real low and my second marriage was at an end and I hated the fact I was going to have to break the news to my eldest daughter, Taylor, that we were going to have to leave while hearing the constant battle of rumours in my head of another shameful failed marriage haunting and echoing continuously. I will never forget her response. She instantly told me that her home is where I am, her Mum. I honestly don't think she truly realises to this day just how much that stuck with me, never mind how much strength it gave me to carry on. She was only about 13 at the time. I'm so grateful for that lesson in life, Taylor, thank you for helping me, more than you will ever truly know.

Hindsight

Hindsight is a wonderful thing because you can reflect and take stock and flourish by lessons in life and grow stronger and overcome any other hurdles that may arise. As I've said before, I have no regrets and I honestly am grateful for my past experiences as there's been lots of silver linings, even amongst lots of heart ache and unnecessary pain, I suppose, but without those experiences how do we grow in life? I believe you're never dealt a hand you can't cope with. Imagine living your life in fear of stepping out of your own comfort zone? Where's the fun in that?

Do something today and tomorrow, no matter how small, that makes you feel alive and slightly challenged. Then, reflect, in hindsight, and see how you feel. Notice intentionally how you can't change it, but you can reflect in a moment, and you can make a new decision, and that's all it takes. It is what it is, and that's how it will stay, unless you change it. If it doesn't serve you, change it.

Smile

I believe that to pass on a smile is one of the most beautiful things you can offer. It can brighten someone's day and make them feel they are not alone. It can brighten your day!

I used to see this woman when I was younger. In my head I used to call her Frosty Face as she always looked so cross and scary. I used to avoid eye contact with her as she had a stare like Medusa, and I thought she would turn me to stone someday. So, this particular day I was in extremely good mood and feeling very happy and nothing was going to upset my day. There I was walking down the street and who pops her head around the corner but Frosty Face. I thought about turning as I couldn't cross the road because of an iron railing. I put on my imaginary big girl pants and strutted towards her, looked her straight in the eye, and said hello with a big exaggerated smile no doubt. She opened her mouth and instead of the expected cyber tooth tiger teeth was a lovely warm cute smile and her eyes softened with it. My heart melted to see the softness in her face. We shared a moment of kindness and warmth between two human beings. I always remember thinking after it that I would never judge like that again. Every time after that when we met, we always gave each other a big smile and, on days I was feeling a bit low her smile always made me feel better. The moral to my story is not to judge and offer your smile instead. I later found out that the lady had lost her childhood sweetheart shortly after they married, they were totally in love and idolised one another. She was carrying their child when he died and shortly after his death, she also lost their first child. She never remarried. Such a tragic story and I never knew it until I was a lot older.

When you smile not only does it help others, it lifts your inner spirit and of course when you receive one, it truly uplifts the soul, especially from a loved one. Smile and what's the worst someone can do? They don't smile back and even then, I'm going to give them the benefit of the doubt and guess they have no teeth. I would love to see everyone smile more, so would you please humour me and give extra three smiles to people that may need it. I'm a great believer when you give you automatically receive.

In hindsight, this taught me a great lesson. At the time I wasn't sure of this lady's journey, but I am so glad I wasn't another person to pass her. The smile reinforced that we were meant to meet and engage in simple smiles as we greeted each other.

Thank you, Lady with the beautiful smile, and I'm grateful we shared lots of engaging smiles together.

The True Power of Gratitude

When you sincerely show gratitude, you will become a more accomplished person and you will find inner strength from something much bigger than us all. I am sure of this.

I give birth to my second daughter, Beth, who I also adore and very proud of. When she was five days old, I had just fed her and was going for a bath straight after while she rested. This day I felt the urge to sit down on the bed and I was looking at her in awe. Now I don't know what made me turn and come back and sit and watch over her, but I am sincerely grateful that I did. She had vomited and was on her back - that's what we were advised to do but not what my Mum would have done. Beth began to choke on her own vomit. I lifted her straight away. I put her on my knee and tried to relieve her, it was not working so I then progressed to putting her down the length of my arm in front of mirror to see if that helped. She started to go blue around her mouth and go limp. My insides were screaming but all I could do was breathe my way through the nightmare and keep calm, while I didn't recognise an on-going whimpering sound that was coming out of me. I rang the ambulance and they stayed on the phone with me and I did what I was asked to do. Beth started to very silently breathe again and for that I'm so ever grateful to the ambulance team that helped me that day. The ambulance arrived and as I greeted them, they checked her over and said we would go to hospital as she was very lifeless. I went to walk and was reminded by the ambulance driver to put some clothes on and I was totally oblivious to the fact that I had only a bra and pants on. I was unconcerned and raced upstairs to grab the first thing I could see and off we went.

People ask about hard times and difficult times and how you get through. This was by far my biggest challenge and I was totally terrified. When I got to the hospital, I passed her over to the consultant and they were amazing and checked her over thoroughly. This is when I broke down and cried so hard that day that she was still living, and I also feared the lack of oxygen to the brain would affect the rest of her life. It was one of the most terrifying experiences in my life as I felt so helpless. I'm so grateful to the staff at the hospital as they were amazing, and I'll never forget what they did for us. My lesson was to give gratitude and listened to my gut. My Beth is a picture of health now and a very gifted child, which shows so much compassion for all around her and she teaches me well daily. She has such a purity and kindness around her.

I ask that you acknowledge ten things that you are grateful for daily, no matter how small and rite them down as I do. Even if you can't write them down, say them in your head on way to work, in the shower or on route to school run. Try this exercise for at least 10 days and when you feel the benefit of these small positive exercises you can implement them daily from then on. Having a healthy beautiful peace of mind and calmness is heavenly and rewarding.

What if our life and our journey in life is our teacher? Have you ever thought about that? What if the test is how we cope with what life throws at us and how we accept and adapt to unwanted change and challenges? I believe there's a bigger presence than us out there and we can draw on the strength it brings. If that concept is not for you, that's okay, but in times of challenge it's important to find someone you look up to and ask for help and let them be your strength or a mentor until you find the belief in yourself. I'm not talking about just anyone, connect with people who are exceptionally good for you. If it's not someone who you truly admire or is excelling in life and can walk the walk or has a QBE (Qualified by Experience), as Donna Kennedy would tell you, I wouldn't be to over excited about their opinions of you. Other people's opinions, unless asked for, are like belly buttons. After you come into this world, they serve no purpose whatsoever and only gather unnecessary dirt and fluff. Note to oneself: "Keep your own belly button clean and to oneself." I believe you're brought into this world to be the best version of yourself, whether you're a loner or a leader, and I feel it's our intentions towards others and how much we appreciate life is that matters most. Appreciate yourself. You are amazing!

I am grateful to you my friend for taking the time to read this book and I can honestly tell you I wish for you to be happy. I am honoured to be assisted, alongside these other beautiful talented ladies, and so grateful to my amazing mentor, Donna Kennedy, who is such a rock for me and such an inspiration and a fountain of knowledge. I am grateful to Donna for helping me see a higher energy in myself and Thankful for her life, and light she shines in this world, and the positive ripple effect that she is applying.

I am very grateful and feel very blessed for my two beautiful daughters Taylor and Beth and to the love of my life, who eventually found me, Jim Brennan. Thank you all for loving me, believing in me and supporting me in all that I do.

Gratitude brings happiness and that's where I am and the heart of the alphabet of life G AND H which of course is Gratitude and Happiness. In the word happiness as you see there is two pp's and two ss's. This to me stands for Perfect Person and She Shone. After H in the alphabet of my life comes I.

I promise to remind myself what lessons I've been taught through my journey so far, and to embrace all things with a mindset of 'Life is the teacher and I am the student'. I look forward to abundant good health, wealth and happiness and many magical experiences and I wish the same for you. Let's face it, life is only a hop, skip and a jump, so let's get hopping, skipping and jumping.

Love always, your new friend, Maria xxx

A Final Note
by Donna Kennedy

And so, it seems that we have come to the end of this book.

Or have we?

Seem is a strange word, isn't it, for what seems is not always what is. Have you ever noticed that when you get good news or win a prize, for example, suddenly the world and the people in it seem so much nicer? People let you out in traffic and you do the same, staff in stores seem nicer, you become more generous etc., yet when you get bad news, everyone seems like they are out to annoy you, when in fact they aren't.

It's not that the world suddenly becomes nicer as a result of your change in mood, it's that it "seems" nicer because you are filtering it differently. As such, we behave differently. It's a bit like wearing sun glasses, the shade of the glass-filter determines your view. If you have pink glasses on, the world seems pink. If you have blue glasses on the world's seems blue etc. The reality is one thing, the perception of it is another. That said, life is not about the circumstances we find ourselves in, so much as how we filter or view our circumstances and how we react to them.

Having read this book your filter (your view of the world) has changed, whether you realise it or not, and it can never be the same again. Your brain has already downloaded new thinking and perspectives, which by default created a new filter. You may even have experienced unexpected or varied emotions during this process. Did you feel "moved" at any point? Remember what I said at the beginning of this book, we only experience emotion when we are moved out of our comfort boxes.

So why am I telling you this now? Very simply, although you may have finished reading this book, you have only started your journey and adventure! Having had your comfort box rattled a bit (that's a good thing!), it's time for something new and wonderful. Deep down you know that your potential is ready for you, just like when you were that excited curious child. You have everything that you need to create the life you want, even if it "seemed" otherwise when you opened this book. If you need to learn skills, so what, learn them. If you need extra help, ask for it, but from this moment on never shy away from your authentic unique brilliance.

You were born with a natural ability to seek out what you need to reach you potential. That ability is, and always will be, within you., even if it was temporarily hidden within the confines of a comfort box. Think about it, when you were a new born baby, you weren't taught to cry when you needed food or affection, you just knew what you needed and did what it took to get it. You still have that inner knowing, just allow yourself to connect with it. Become the director of your life. It's time. You are not alone anymore. *WE Summit Together!*

Love Donna xxx

For information about events and where to find us

please go to **www.wesummit.ie**

Acknowledgements

- I wish to acknowledge the following people for their dedication, support and eagerness to empower others.

- Co-Authors: Lucy Carty, Melanie Ardoin, Maria Farkasova, Aoife Gaffney, Liz Dillon-Valloor, Jennifer Clarke, Jenny McSweeney, Niamh Duffy, Tracey McCann, Marie Donnery, Martina O'Riordan, Jennifer Byrne and Maria Farrell. It is a privilege to have these ladies in the world.

- Pat Slattery (www.patslattery.com) for being the kindest, most loving and supportive life-partner I could ask for. I love him with all my heart.

- Christina Noble. Her love, strength and courage have inspired and impacted my approach to life.

- Jean Murtagh (The Christina Noble Children's Foundation). She is a true gem and it is a pleasure to know her.

- The Women's Empowerment Summit (WE Summit) events team (www.wesummit.ie). Thank you for all the work you do. Thank you to Damian Moloney (eventhost.ie) for taking the lead when needed.

- Rafal Kostrzewa (www.dublinheadshot.com) for his professionalism and attention to detail.

- Deleyo Design for their creativity and vision.

- Steven Kontra (Webstop www.webstop.ie) for website design and support

About the Authors

Donna Kennedy is a four-times bestselling author and international professional speaker. She has been endorsed by some of the largest organizations in the world and her academic work has been published for university research and reference.

"Listen to this girl. She knows what she's talking about"
-Bob Proctor." (The Secret)

"It was a privilege to share the stage with such a great speaker as Donna Kennedy" – Brian Tracy (Goals)

Niamh Duffy is a loving wife and mother of two children. Her interest in helping and empowering others is evident in all she does. By profession she is a school secretary and a trainee yoga instructor, but her reach goes beyond any formal education. Niamh's personality oozes love, and you cannot but be impacted by her kind personality and approach to life.

Jennifer Clarke was born in Dublin and is a mum of three children and wife to Darren. She works in the pharmaceutical industry and is a self-confessed nerd. She empowers women by helping them to understand the importance of self-acceptance. She also has single handily managed to keep all shoe shops in business due to her obsession with shoes!

Tracey McCann had her world turned upside down at the age of eight, when she was struck with a disability known as rapid onset muscular Dystonia which subsequently affected her ability to verbally communicate. Now in her thirties, Tracey is a bestselling author, international inspirational speaker, life coach and disabled advocate.

Maria Farkasova works in Human Resources and is currently studying towards her diploma. She loves travelling and is passionate about self-development. She holds several qualifications, including life and executive coaching, mBIT and NLP, and she has a Masters Degree in International Trade.

Jennifer Byrne has a BA in Modern Languages (Double Hons). She is a registered sports nutritionist, lifestyle coach, and personal trainer. She empowers others to be the healthiest, happiest version of themselves from the inside out. Through her extensive knowledge within the health and fitness industry and life experiences she provides the tools to implement sustainable, healthier lifestyle practices.

Lucy Carty was raised on a small farm in Roscommon. She is a qualified nurse and owner of *Eden Skin and Laser Clinic*. Living in and loving the West of Ireland she is a passionate networker and founded the Roscommon branch of Network Ireland for women in business and the Groom the Goddess Event. Lucy is a firm believer in finding her tribe to empower herself and others. She is a rescuer of one German Sheperd and mother to the two "most handsomest sons ever."

Jenny McSweeney is a life and success coach and founded *New Perspective* which helps people see a new way to build confidence and have success in many areas in life. She will inspire and empower you to the point where you are convinced you are nothing short of amazing.

Marie Donnery is a mother of six adult children and a grandmother of fifteen grandchildren. She has been busy working on herself over the years while rearing her family, and has several qualifications in holistic therapies, including facilitation, life coaching, KI Massage Therapy and Reiki. She is passionate about helping people through nature by quieting their busy mind to unleash their hero from within.

Liz Dillon-Valloor is an author and international speaker. She has facilitated workshops and retreats at the Sadhana Institute in India, Notre Dame in the USA and the Theosophical Society in Auckland.

Melanie Ardoin is a Global Program Manager and Consultant and a mum of two children. She also coaches people going though divorce/ separation and single parents. Her multi-faceted understanding and life experiences has allowed her to create positive change for many people.

Aoife Gaffney MSc (Hons) BSc (Open) QFA LIB CMC is the founder of *Prudence Moneypenny Coaching*, a unique coaching programme designed to empower women to take control of their financial freedom. She is a Certified Money Coach, NLP practitioner, Qualified Financial Adviser, bestselling author and speaker. Her approach to all things money is holistic, compassionate and humorous. She deals with a serious subject in a light-hearted way and speaks from personal experience.

Martina O'Riordan is the owner of *MartinaO Weddings & Events* (www.martinao.com). She is a Wedding Planner and Stylist based in Ireland with over ten years' events and marketing experience from both Ireland and abroad. Her recent wedding featured in Vogue, highlighting her dedication to assisting couples abroad get married in Ireland and making the process as streamlined as possible for them. Martina is an executor and is passionate about the challenge of bringing each couple's unique story to life.

Maria Farrell was born in Strabane and is qualified in dog training and behaviour. Owner of *Paw Doggy Day Care* and *Little Paws South Down Kids Training*, Maria has a fun live-life-to-the-max personality, which helps others rise above the daily grind and enjoy their purpose.

All book sale profits go to
The Christina Noble Children's Foundation

Christina Noble, OBE, has by her own effort and example and with an unselfish willingness to serve, shown the world that street children are a vital part of humanity – that the abuse and maltreatment suffered by children can be stopped. Born into the slums of Dublin, Ireland, Christina overcame the death of her mother at an early age and spent her childhood in dire circumstances - surviving years spent in industrial schools and a period of homelessness. Her difficult beginnings fuelled her passion for children's rights, to which she has dedicated her life. In 1997, Christina travelled to Mongolia and saw first-hand the deprivation left behind after the withdrawal of the Soviet Union and the socio-economic collapse of the country. Christina expanded CNCF's operations to help the thousands of children forced to live in the manholes of the dilapidated freezing streets of Ulaanbaatar. Christina is the author of two international best-selling autobiographies, *Bridge Across My Sorrows* and *Mama Tina* and was also the subject of three award-winning documentaries and the biopic feature NOBLE (2014), which won seven international film awards.

Printed in Poland
by Amazon Fulfillment
Poland Sp. z o.o., Wrocław